☆

Mem Fox was born in Melbourne, grew up in Africa, studied drama in England, and returned to Australia in 1970.

She is the highly regarded author of more than thirty books for young children, including *Time for Bed, Where Is the Green Sheep?*, and *Possum Magic,* which is the bestselling picture book ever in Australia. She has also written five nonfiction books for adults.

She was a professor in literacy studies at Flinders University in South Australia, where she taught teachers for twenty-four years until her early retirement in 1996. She is now an influential international literacy consultant and has received many civic awards and honors for her work in literacy.

Mem lives in Adelaide with her husband and an old dog. Their daughter, Chloë, lives close by.

☆

Visit Mem Fox at www.memfox.com.

Reading Magic

BOOKS BY MEM FOX

For children

A Bedtime Story

Boo to a Goose

Feathers and Fools

Guess What?

*Harriet,
You'll Drive Me Wild!*

Hattie and the Fox

Hunwick's Egg

Koala Lou

The Magic Hat

Night Noises

A Particular Cow

Possum Magic

Shoes from Grandpa

Sleepy Bears

Sophie

The Straight Line Wonder

Time for Bed

Tough Boris

Where Is the Green Sheep?

Where the Giant Sleeps

Whoever You Are

*Wilfrid Gordon
McDonald Partridge*

Wombat Divine

Zoo Looking

For adults

*Dear Mem Fox, I Have Read All Your Books
Even the Pathetic Ones and Other Incidents in the Life
of a Children's Book Author*

*English Essentials: The Wouldn't-Be-Without-It Guide
to Writing Well* (cowritten with Lyn Wilkinson)

*Radical Reflections: Passionate Opinions
on Teaching, Learning, and Living*

Teaching Drama to Young Children

MEM FOX

Reading Magic

☆

Why Reading Aloud
to Our Children Will Change
Their Lives Forever

Updated and Revised Edition

Illustrations by Judy Horacek

A HARVEST ORIGINAL
HARCOURT, INC.
Orlando   Austin   New York   San Diego   London

Requests for permission to make copies of any part of the
work should be submitted online at www.harcourt.com/contact
or mailed to the following address: Permissions Department,
Houghton Mifflin Harcourt Publishing Company,
6277 Sea Harbor Drive, Orlando, Florida 32887-6777.

www.HarcourtBooks.com

Excerpts from *Koula Lou*, text copyright © 1988 by Mem Fox, reprinted
by permission of Harcourt, Inc.; excerpts from *Night Noises*, text copyright
© 1989 by Mem Fox, reprinted by permission of Harcourt, Inc.; excerpt
from *Wombat Divine*, text copyright © 1995 by Mem Fox, reprinted by
permission of Harcourt, Inc.; excerpt from *Hattie and the Fox*, text copyright © 1986 by Mem Fox, reprinted by permission of Simon & Schuster
Books for Young Readers, an imprint of Simon & Schuster Children's
Publishing Division; excerpt from *Wilfrid Gordon McDonald Partridge*, text
copyright © 1985 by Mem Fox, reprinted by permission of Kane/Miller
Book Publishers; excerpts from *Harriet, You'll Drive Me Wild!*, text copyright © 2000 by Mem Fox, reprinted by permission of Harcourt, Inc.; excerpt from *Sleepy Bears*, text copyright © 1999 by Mem Fox, reprinted by
permission of Harcourt, Inc.; excerpt from *Possum Magic*, text copyright ©
1983 by Mem Fox, reprinted by permission of Harcourt, Inc.; excerpt
from *Feathers and Fools*, text copyright © 1989 by Mem Fox, reprinted by
permission of Harcourt, Inc.; *Tough Boris*, text copyright © 1994 by Mem
Fox, reprinted by permission of Harcourt, Inc.; excerpt from *Hattie and the
Fox* (Indonesian language edition) by Mem Fox, illustrated by Patricia
Mullins, text copyright © Mem Fox, 1986, translation by Trina Supit,
first published by Scholastic Australia Pty Ltd 1995, reprinted by permission of Scholastic Australia Pty Ltd; excerpt from *The Wedding Ghost*, text
copyright © Leon Garfield 1985, reprinted by permission of John John-
son (Author's Agent) Limited; excerpts from *Time for Bed*, text copyright
© 1993 by Mem Fox, reprinted by permission of Harcourt, Inc.

Library of Congress Cataloging-in-Publication Data
Fox, Mem, 1946–
Reading magic: why reading aloud to our children will change their lives
forever/Mem Fox; illustrations by Judy Horacek.—Updated and rev. ed.
p.   cm.
1. Storytelling   2. Oral reading.   3. Children—Books and reading.
I. Title.
LB1042.F64   2008
372.67'7—dc22   2008005627
ISBN 978-0-15-603510-1

Designed by Linda Lockowitz
Text set in Meridien

Printed in the United States of America
Second edition
A C E G H F D B

For Jim Trelease,
King of the Read-Alouds

☆

Contents

☆

Foreword

I'm excited! Since *Reading Magic* was first published in 2001, reading aloud to young children has taken off in ways I'd never dreamt possible. Rather than being viewed as a mildly pleasant educational activity, it feels now as if the entire world is in a frenzy about reading aloud, for a variety of reasons. The mood has changed. Attitudes have altered. Even the perceived benefits have expanded, especially in the realm of brain development. "Reading aloud" is a buzz phrase around Australia and internationally. Everyone's excited, not just me.

In the last few years I've listened to or worked with many people who are passionate about spreading the read-aloud message from their own standpoint: pediatricians, speech pathologists, child psychologists, social workers, librarians, economists, childcare workers, bookstore owners, politicians, teachers and researchers, carers, media personalities, parents, and other passionate individuals. Every person, every group, and every government official I met was, and still is, working hard to bring home the message that reading aloud to children before they start school is a win/win situation for all concerned.

It all boils down to economics in the end, which is a little dry, I'll admit. But the idea is that reading aloud to our babies and young children will make the entire country better off. Governments now realize that by providing attention, time, and funds to promoting early literacy, less of their budgets later will need to be spent on illiteracy, crime, depression, unemployment, and welfare benefits. The cost-effectiveness of reading aloud to the very young is phenomenal, and governments love that kind of read-aloud news.

It stands to reason that if we're able to raise happier, brighter children by reading aloud to them, the well-being of the entire country will ramp up a notch. Children who realize in their first few weeks and months of life that listening to stories is the purest heaven; who understand that books are filled with delights, facts, fun, and food for thought; who fall in love with their parents, and their parents with them, while stories are being shared; and who are read aloud to for ten minutes a day in their first five years, usually learn to read quickly, happily, and easily. And a whole lot of goodness follows for the entire community. Great news, isn't it? No wonder I can't contain myself.

Since *Reading Magic* was first published, two topics in particular have consistently grabbed headlines: phonics, and boys and reading. Both are of huge concern to parents. I mentioned them several times in the first edition, but not in depth. I'm delighted to be able to discuss them in greater detail in two new chapters in this edition.

I've also included for the first time a list of twenty classics that babies, young children, and you will adore.

Now let's get on and change the world, one page at a time.

—Mem Fox

CHAPTER ONE

☆

The Foot Book Miracle

In 1975 our daughter, Chloë, came home from school in a state of excitement and said, "I can read!" She was four years old and had been at school for two weeks. We smiled indulgently as parents do when they think their child is cute. Read? She had to be joking.

She ran to her room and came back with *The Foot Book* by Dr. Seuss, one of her favorites at the time, and read it to us word for word, with expression. We were beside ourselves.

But could she *really* read? We had read that book to her so many times, we thought she might have memorized it. We hesitated, not wanting to dampen her wild enthusiasm, then bravely opened the book at random to see if she could read a page by itself, without reciting the whole book by rote from the beginning. She read that page, and another page at random, and another.

At the time, I was a college professor teaching drama. I knew nothing about the teaching of reading. In my eyes I was "only" a mother. I rushed to Chloë's school the next morning and told her teacher what had happened.

"What did you do?" I asked, agog. "What method did you use? It's a miracle!"

"I didn't do much," she said. "How could I? She's only been in my class for two weeks. You must have read to her often before she came to school."

"Of course," I said.

"Well, there you go," said the teacher, as if that were that.

From that moment I became fascinated by the benefits of reading aloud. The seeds were sown for a change in my teaching career—out of drama into literacy. If reading aloud had had such a powerful impact on my child's life and on her ability to learn to read, I felt I had no business keeping it a secret. I had to spread the word.

☆

horacek

Over the last twenty-five years, I've learned a great deal more about how children learn to read and write and about the many other positive effects of reading aloud to children. I now travel the world, talking to parents, teachers, librarians, and booksellers, urging everyone I meet to read aloud to the children in their lives—and explaining why. I speak with the authority of an international literacy consultant and the intensity of a writer, but I'm most passionate when I speak as an ordinary mother. Reading aloud to my daughter was a fabulous experience. We bonded through all sorts of marvelous books. We came to know and love each other better through the variety of stories we shared. I hadn't realized that reading aloud regularly would mean Chloë would learn to read without being taught.

It was enough just to be together.

☆

The Magic in Action

A few years ago I was involved in the filming of a national television program about the benefits of reading aloud to preschoolers. It was suggested that I speak on camera to the mother and father of a three-year-old about why parents should read to their children.

These particular parents were keen to do their very best for their little boy, but they had rarely read to him and had not realized the importance of doing so. He couldn't read or write a word.

On the day in question, I was startled to find that I wouldn't be chatting with the parents, after all. Instead, the director wanted me to read to the child so I could demonstrate the loving, riotous, joyful reading-aloud atmosphere I'd been advocating earlier in the program.

I don't know this child! I thought. *I've never met him in my life! I'll terrify him with my overwhelming personality. How can he and I be friends and learn to read happily together, just like that, with a snap of the fingers and no prior relationship?*

We were all a little edgy and pressured by lack of time, though I did manage to extricate Ben (not his real name) from the cameras and the lights for a minute or two so we could walk out to my car together, hand in hand, and share in private the special gifts I had brought him: a poster from my new book *Time for Bed* and the book itself.

A few moments later, lying on the floor of his living room with the cameras rolling, I read to him. Then I read with him. And then *he read to me.* All this happened in fifteen minutes.

The night before the program was due to be televised nationally, there was an ad for it that almost caused me to have a seizure. It said something along these lines: "THIS WOMAN CLAIMS SHE CAN TEACH YOUR BABY TO READ IN FIFTEEN MINUTES!" Of course I hadn't claimed any such thing. To have done so would have been preposterous.

But it is true that within fifteen minutes of my reading aloud to Ben, he put his fingers under the correct words, grinned a cheeky grin, and said, "It's time for bed." The cameraman gasped. The soundman leaned forward. The director did a little dance. The parents were stunned into disbelieving silence.

Even I thought it had been an accident, so I turned over to another page and said, "And what do we have on *this* page?" Once again Ben put his podgy little finger under the words, and laughing his head off, he said, "It's time for bed." And when I turned to another page, he did the same thing yet again. It was all recorded on camera. He had *begun* to learn to read in fifteen minutes—this normal child of normal parents, none of whom I had met before.

☆

To explain Ben's success in this situation, I could say that I used over and over again three very simple picture books: my own *Time for Bed* and *Hattie and the Fox,* and Pamela Allen's *Who Sank the Boat?* That would be the truth. I could also say I chose them because they each had the same animals and they each had the important elements of rhyme, rhythm, or repetition. That would also be the truth.

But the most significant truth, I believe, is what

happened between me and the child. There was a frenzy of silliness and excited game playing, with me shouting and laughing and saying, "Yes! Yes! Yes!" in higher and higher tones, and hugging Ben, who was laughing and grinning as if this reading thing were just about the best fun he'd ever had. We were literally rolling around on the floor and banging the book with our hands at each new revelation of "It's time for bed," shrieking in triumph as the words were revealed on each page.

We were never tense. We were never quiet. Even when we were looking for and finding the same farm animals in each book, we were noisy and wild in our discoveries—and in our togetherness.

"There's *another* pig! Oh no! *Another* horse! And look, there's a cow in this book, and a cow in this book, and another cow in *this* book! Can you believe it? Cows, cows, everywhere!"

Ben's face was alight. I could have eaten him, he was so adorable and so bright-eyed; and he thought I was pretty special, too. Every time I lifted him off the floor in a giant hug and said, "Ooh, you're so *clever*!" he was mesmerized with happiness. We could have played with books for hours. We didn't want to stop. Good grief! How happy we were!

Is it any wonder that three-year-old Ben was re-

laxed enough to *begin* to learn to read in fifteen
minutes and to want to go on learning? For him the
rewards were manifold. He loved the game we
played because I made sure he was always "win-
ning." The books themselves were fun, with all their
rowdy, rhythmic language and their crazily repetitive words reappearing page after page. But best of

all, he had a good time with a new friend: me. We were mates.

☆

Engaging in this kind of conspiracy with children is perhaps the greatest benefit of reading aloud to them. As we share the words and pictures, the ideas and viewpoints, the rhythms and rhymes, the pain and comfort, and the hopes and fears and big issues of life that we encounter together in the pages of a book, we connect through minds and hearts with our children and bond closely in a secret society associated with the books we have shared. The fire of literacy is created by the emotional sparks between a child, a book, and the person reading. It isn't achieved by the book alone, nor by the child alone, nor by the adult who's reading aloud—it's the relationship winding between all three, bringing them together in easy harmony.

☆

Reading aloud shouldn't be thought of as a grimacing This Is Good for Your Child event for mothers and fathers. When we get involved in reading aloud to our babies and other children, we often forget entirely that we *should* be reading aloud. We have such a rollicking good time, and we relate so warmly to our kids as we read together, that it becomes a delicious "chocolate" kind of experience.

"Chocolate" happened for my hairdresser. Her daughter Tiffy, a sassy piece of dynamite, was reading with great expression and verve to the entire neighborhood at the age of barely six, and everyone said to her mother, "You must have taught her. She's so far ahead."

"Taught her?" said her mother. "Of course I didn't teach her. I wouldn't know how, and I wouldn't have dared anyway, in case I did something wrong. All I did was read aloud."

Her friends didn't believe her. It just seemed too easy.

☆

Children won't always learn to read before they start school even if we do read aloud to them, and that's absolutely fine. Teachers will, with grateful hearts, build on the solid reading-aloud foundation provided by us (and by nannies or day care providers) prior to school, and those children will very quickly learn how to read for themselves.

But if every parent understood the huge educational benefits and intense happiness brought about by reading aloud to their children, and if every parent—and every adult caring for a child—read aloud a minimum of three stories a day to the children in their lives, we could probably wipe out illiteracy within one generation.

What's to stop us? Let's give it a go!

CHAPTER THREE

☆

Birth, Brains, and Beyond

Reading problems are difficult to fix but very easy to prevent. Prevention happens *long before a child starts school*. In fact, the first day of school is almost too late for a child to begin to learn to read. It's as scary as that.

Recent brain research has revealed that the early years of life are more critical to a child's development than we ever realized. Children's brains are only 25 percent developed at birth. From that moment, whenever a baby is fed, cuddled, played with, talked to, sung to, or read to, the other 75 percent of its brain begins to develop. And the more stimulation the baby has through its senses of touch, taste, smell, sight, and hearing, the more rapidly that development will occur. It's as if the brain were an excited acrobat learning fantastic tricks with every new piece of information, with every scrap of new stimulation. Amazing though it may seem, the crucial connections that determine how clever, creative, and imaginative a child will be are already laid down by the time that child turns one.

And by the age of one, children will have also learned all the sounds that make up the native languages they are going to speak. This is why we can't speak the languages that we learn later in life with flawless accents; we don't have the right wires laid down in our brains and connected early enough. Hence the difficulty English speakers have with the *r* sound in French and the tones in Chinese, and the difficulty Japanese speakers have with the *r* sound in English—and the difficulty any of us has when we try to learn a foreign language as late as the age of twelve. Since learning to read is rather like learning a foreign language, we need to establish the "native" language of books (for example, the more formal grammar found in stories and the conventions of "Once upon a time" and "They all lived happily ever after") in that important first year, to inoculate children against illiteracy, in the same way that we inoculate them against measles and polio.

The foundations of learning to read are set down from the moment a child first hears the sounds of people talking, the tunes of songs, and the rhythms and repetitions of rhymes and stories. Children who have not been regularly talked to, sung to, or read aloud to from birth find life at school much more burdensome than they otherwise might. In particular, learning to read becomes a major stumbling block rather than a surprising delight.

☆

Reading aloud to children early in life also rapidly develops their speaking skills. They don't learn to talk—they can't learn to talk—unless they're spoken to, which is why psychologists and speech pathologists tell us we need to have loving, laughing, deep-and-meaningful conversations with our kids long before they turn three. These conversations have also been linked positively to IQ development. The more we talk to our kids, the brighter they'll be.

Read-aloud sessions are perfect times for engaging in these sorts of conversations because the reader and the listener can chat endlessly about the story, the pictures, the words, the values, and the ideas. Reading aloud and talking about what we're reading sharpens children's brains. It helps develop their ability to concentrate at length, to solve problems logically, and to

express themselves more easily and clearly. The stories they hear provide them with witty phrases, new sentences, and words of subtle meaning.

Before long children begin to understand the look of the print and the way words work in sentences, and how the world works—why this happens and that happens—and how it all comes together to mean something. In other words, they learn to read.

No wonder experts tell us that children need to hear a thousand stories read aloud before they begin to learn to read for themselves. A thousand! That sounds daunting. But when we do the sums, it isn't as bad as we might think. Three stories a day will deliver us a thousand stories in one year alone, let alone in the four or five years prior to school. We can do it!

The ideal three stories a day are one favorite, one familiar, and one new, but the same book three times is also fine. I had coffee recently with a friend who is a besotted grandfather. That morning his two-year-old granddaughter, Niav, had demanded that he read the same picture book over and over again for forty minutes. In that one read-aloud session, they were well on their way to the recommended thousand books.

☆

Because words are essential in building the thought connections in the brain, the more language a child experiences—through books and through conversation with others, *not passively from television*—the more advantaged socially, educationally, and in every way that child will be for the rest of his or her life. Conversely, the fewer words a child experiences, learns, and uses before school, the more stunted that child's brain will be.

Many people believe that television provides enough language for children to learn to talk. It's true that programs like the *Book Place* in Australia and *Reading Rainbow* in the United States have great merit because they teach children about stories and how they work, which is an important foundation for reading. But the worrisome aspect of television is that it doesn't develop children's ability to speak, even when it's an educational program—in spite of all the words that pour out of it. Television doesn't talk to children—it talks at them and they can't talk back, and *talking back* is what learning language is all about.

A friend of mine with an eleven-month-old son has picture books lying around the house for him to look at alone anytime, as well as treasured autographed hardcover copies that she keeps out of reach. When she says, "Ryan, shall we get down the special books?" he's beside himself with anticipation. He almost trembles because he knows that when the special books come down, he and his mother will read them together, and he'll have his mother's full attention as they talk about this and that in the stories they're reading. Because of this interaction, it's unlikely that Ryan will ever need the services of a speech pathologist. He's encouraged to *talk back,* in his own way, even at eleven months.

Dr. Sue Hill, an expert in early childhood at the University of South Australia, says bonding and literacy development happen even when we read—and talk about—ordinary things with our children, such as Christmas catalogs, cereal boxes, and magazines. Of course, simple, intriguing books—like *Where's Spot?* by Eric Hill, for example—are more fun and more interesting for a young child, but any print will do as long as that child has a chance to *talk back.*

Eamon, the son of my editor, Allyn Johnston, has the opportunity to *talk back* about postcards. Allyn travels a lot for work and sends him postcards from the places she goes. Eamon looks for them in the mail, and he and his dad read them together for comfort while she's gone. The postcards become a topic of conversation. His dad talks about them and Eamon *talks back* to him. From these postcards Eamon is also learning why we read: as he sees the print, he realizes that its purpose is to send a real message from one person to another.

☆

It's hard to find time to really talk with our children. We all know that twenty-first-century living is more than hectic. For parents whose careers eat time and endanger relationships—and I emphasize busy fathers as well as busy mothers—the read-aloud session between a parent and child is one of the most effective rescue remedies available. The time spent reading together provides clear evidence to a child of a parent's love, care, and focused attention. And it gives the parent a chance to close off the rest of the world, relax, and connect with the child wonderfully.

One of the unsung but cozy effects of reading aloud is the private language that develops in families through shared book experience. Chloë and I went on a picnic once when she was six, and she asked—even before we'd unpacked the basket—what we were having for "afters." I told her there was more sensible food to be eaten before "afters" could even be considered.

"Well, one must sustain oneself," she said, in a six-year-old huff.

The phrase had come directly from *Winnie-the-Pooh*. Over time it became one of the standard sayings in our family, especially when my husband, Malcolm, had eaten all the chocolate in the house.

"Well, one must sustain oneself," he'd say, with a guilty look.

We were knitted into the same familial fabric by a book language that meant nothing to people outside our immediate little trio. It was a private "togetherness" code that connected us all.

☆

The sense of dislocation and confusion that occurs when kids and parents don't connect disturbs children long after childhood is over. In his brilliant book *The Uses of Enchantment,* renowned child psychologist Bruno Bettelheim tells us bluntly that children need to know above all that they're loved by their parents. No matter how much they are loved by their grandparents, nannies, or others, the love children crave most is the love of their parents. And parents can show that love by giving children time—it may be as little as fifteen minutes a day—to read aloud together, to talk to each other, and to bond.

When Chloë was well into adulthood, I asked nervously if she felt she'd been ignored as a child with

all my frantic juggling of two careers and the responsibilities of home. She was startled.

"Wasn't I the center of your world?" she asked.

"Did you feel you were?" I said.

"Of course. I *was* the center of your world,
wasn't I?"

"Yes, yes, you were," I said hastily.

"Well, what are you getting at?"

"Oh, nothing . . ."

Somehow, in all the rush and madness surrounding her childhood, she'd picked up the idea that she
was my central focus. Truly she had been adored—
and is—but from where exactly had she been able to
pluck the knowledge that she'd mattered more to me
and Malcolm than anyone else in the universe?

In large part, it was from the times we'd read
aloud to her at night. We were in our own space at
those times, chatting about the books, comparing them
to other stories, empathizing with Eeyore in *Winnie-
the-Pooh* about the general lack of "bonhomie" in his
life, using new words like *soporific* from the *Peter Rab-
bit* stories, being shocked about the last little duck
getting spanked yet again in *The Story about Ping*, gos-
siping without shame about the people we knew who

horacek

were like characters in the books, discussing the Great Questions of Life as they arose in the dilemmas and decisions we encountered, reliving memories, weighing right from wrong, evil from good. And then after we had talked back and forth, she'd snuggle in tight and fall asleep with a head full of thinking, a heart at peace, and a brain on fire with the excitement of books.

CHAPTER FOUR

☆

The Power

So great is the power of reading aloud that Moreen Fielden, headmistress of the Gillispie School, a private elementary school in San Diego, reads aloud to her entire school every Friday. She believes so strongly in the enormous educational benefits it bestows on her students that she used to read aloud to the whole school every *day* until—to her regret—the level of her administrative load made it impossible.

Contrast that with the story of an ignorant principal in New Hampshire who came into a classroom to watch a teacher in action for the purposes of an appraisal and saw that the teacher was reading aloud to her students.

"I'll come back later," he whispered, "when you're *teaching*."

☆

There's no doubt that reading aloud teaches. And there's no doubt that little kids—and big ones—love being read aloud to. Colin Thiele, the beloved Australian children's author, grew up in the Barossa Valley in South Australia and attended a one-teacher school in an area prone to flooding. On flood days, when half the children couldn't make it to school, the teacher—not wanting to "waste" her curriculum on so few children—would spend the day reading aloud. Flood days were magical for Colin. He claims he learned more about reading and writing by accident on those days than he did during the entire rest of the year.

Roald Dahl, the celebrated British writer of *Charlie and the Chocolate Factory* and other wonderful children's and adult fiction, also claimed that being read to was his happiest memory of boarding school and that it taught him more about writing than formal English lessons were ever able to achieve. On Saturday mornings the matron would read aloud to the boarders who weren't able to go home on the weekends—to keep them occupied and out of trouble—thus providing two hours of enchantment each week in an otherwise loveless establishment.

☆

When I was teaching, I would often start the year by reading aloud a children's novel in my first lecture to would-be teachers, to practice what I intended to preach. The students ranged in age from seventeen to forty-five, but their eyes would be round with fascination while I read, nevertheless. Even the football players in my classes loved being read aloud to. They'd sit like silent mice, rapt in spite of themselves, drawn in by the pull of the story.

One of the novels I used to read was *Stone Fox* by John Gardiner. Toward the end of the book, at the point where something unexpectedly terrible happens, there would be a collective gasp in the room. And when I finished reading, the end of the story had such an impact that there would be total silence.

When I meet my ex-students, they often tell me that what they remember most about my classes is the reading aloud: the fun of it and the importance of it. One of them said, "Honestly, Mem, if you walked by my classroom one day and I wasn't reading aloud to my kids, I'd be terrified you'd open the door, walk in, and take over the lesson!"

☆

Then there's Jonas, a little boy I heard about at a school in Illinois. He was in a class for children whose home lives indicated they might need extra help to learn to read and write, and he had a passionate and brilliant teacher who had been working with young children for over thirty years with great success. Jonas adored his teacher. He especially loved listening to the stories she read.

She read aloud to her students many times a day. She knew it made them happier. And cleverer. In particular, she recognized the calming effects of reading aloud when kids were climbing the walls. She would read to them until one by one they peeled themselves off the walls, crept close, and sat in silence at her feet, soothed by the rhythm of the words and spellbound by their magic.

One day after Jonas had been severely provoked by another child, he reacted violently, in a manner unusual for him, and stuck a pencil into the other child's arm. The teacher, in shock, marched him down to the principal's office, a tactic she used rarely in her class, and never before with Jonas. His misdemeanor was explained to the principal and punishment was sought to fit the crime.

"What do *you* suggest, Jonas?" asked the teacher.

Jonas was by now howling with grief and remorse.

"What do you think might be a suitable punishment?" the teacher asked again.

Finally, through his sobs Jonas said, "I guess...I guess...I guess you could stop reading aloud to me."

CHAPTER FIVE

☆

Keep It Regular

The best time to start reading aloud to a baby is the day it is born. The lilting rhythm of a simple bedtime book on that first thrilling, exhausting day is soothing for the tremulous parents and the new child and adds to the bonding between them. It gives them something to "talk about" together. And much to the surprise of most adults, babies love books. They respond to the brightness of the pictures, to the rhythm of the words, and to the presence of a loving adult.

Paula, one of my neighbors, has a six-month-old baby named Monica. When I asked her how Monica was doing, Paula told me she *loved* her books. I thought Paula was teasing. She knows how crazy I am about babies and books.

"No, no, really!" said Paula. "She loves them. She smiles and waves her arms and makes little noises and gets a funny sort of concentrated look whenever we sit down in this particular chair and I start to read. She adores her books, honestly. I'm not kidding."

At six months! I didn't start reading to Chloë until she was ten months because I believed back then that that was early enough. Think of the time I wasted!

☆

With babies, it doesn't even have to be a children's book that we read. One of my teacher education students had a baby she hadn't planned who arrived at an awkward time in her college course. Obviously, this cut down on the time she had available to read, so she decided to read aloud the articles and books I'd set for the semester. The baby never knew the difference. He was lulled by the sound of his mother's calming voice and by the comforting knowledge that she was there with him.

☆

Reading aloud from birth, as my student did to her baby, prevents several reading problems from arising. For example, a parent who knew of the importance of reading aloud once complained to me that her child wouldn't sit still for books.

"He just won't settle down for a story," she said.

Perhaps she didn't start reading aloud soon enough in her son's life. Children who are read to early and regularly quickly acquire the skill of listening and the desire to hear stories. They understand the immense pleasures waiting for them in books and develop the ability to concentrate and relax.

If children don't learn early on how to concentrate for the entire length of a story—or why—they'll never settle down for a book. Boys especially will often fidget and squirm, let their minds latch on to a hundred other things, interrupt too often, or run around. So the earlier we start, the better.

Hunter—the grandson of a friend of mine—was read to from a very early age. By the time he was two, he was able to concentrate on "reading" five or six books to himself at night, before his parents came in to read aloud to him. Books engaged him to such an extent that he had no desire to fidget or squirm.

☆

If birth is the right time of life to start reading aloud, when is the right time of day? Whenever possible and as often as possible. We should make sure, for instance, that we have favorite books with us in situations when it's clear our children might be bored, anxious, whining, irritable, or disruptive. Books take the tedium out of waiting for the doctor; going on a bus, train, or plane journey; sitting around waiting for a parent at the hairdresser's or at the dentist's or at a meeting or a friend's place. Books cool things down when children have been upset by arguments or yelling. Books cheer them when they're ill. Books stop them from being fretful in situations when we need them to be well behaved, such as in church or while we are eating out or visiting relatives and friends.

And then of course there must be books at home. My editor, knowing that she and her son will be apart during the day and feeling sad about it, reads aloud to Eamon before he gets out of bed in the morning so they can have some special time together. I'd never heard of such a routine and could scarcely believe it when she told me. When Chloë was young, our house was always chaos in the morning—one long shouting match until we were all out the door. But every family has its own routines, and what works for one may create havoc in another. We do what's right for us. It's doing it that's important.

☆

Although a read-aloud session can happen anytime, it's important also to have a ritual about reading aloud every night, in the same place, at the same time, with the same cushions or pillows, the same stuffed animals, and the same books. According to Margaret Mead, the noted anthropologist, children not only appreciate the safety of a predictable life, they actually need regular routines to feel secure in the world. So while read-aloud sessions can happen at any time, they *must* happen at bedtime.

If we begin skimping on reading aloud before bed, it may slip from the family routine altogether.

Other things may start to seem more pressing. But what could be more important than our children's literacy and the loving interactions that occur during a read-aloud session? Is feeling too tired a valid excuse? Surely not. The price of *not* reading aloud is too high.

☆

It's beneficial to continue reading aloud to children for as long as they'll let us, even after they can finally read themselves. One of my university teachers read to her children until they were in their late teens. She read books and poems they might not have been drawn to on their own—and they loved it!

Most people, if asked the best time to read aloud to adolescent boys, would probably say *never*! But they would be wrong. My favorite book on reading aloud to the older child—*Better than Life* by Daniel Pennac—explains why. Its focus is adolescents, mainly boys, who've been turned off reading altogether. In an elegant and moving manner, Pennac explains how he switches his students back into loving books and reading. What's his secret?

Reading aloud.

☆

CHAPTER SIX

And Do It Like This

An American father once said to me: "So how do you do this read-aloud thing?" I was almost too taken aback to answer. Wasn't it obvious? Then I realized it wouldn't be obvious if he hadn't been read aloud to as a child. I wanted to say: "Well, you know—find a book, get a child, and sit down and read the book to the child." But it seemed so simple, I was too embarrassed to say it.

When I see a read-aloud session in my mind's eye, there's either an adult sitting in a big old chair or on a sofa, with a child on the adult's lap or snuggled up close, sharing a book, or an adult sitting or lying on a bed with the child tucked in, wide-eyed, as stories are being read. And the experience is always fantastic.

The more expressively we read, the more fantastic the experience will be. The more fantastic the experience, the more our kids will love books, and the more they'll "pretend" read. And the more they "pretend" read, the quicker they'll learn to read. So reading aloud is not quite enough—we need to read aloud *well*.

There's no exact right way of reading aloud, other than to try to be as expressive as possible. As we read a story, we need to be aware of our body position, our eyes and their expression, our eye contact with the child or children, our vocal variety, and our general facial animation. But each of us will have our own special way of doing it. For instance, when I read the beginning of my book *Koala Lou*, my voice swings up and down in the same tune, the same s-l-o-w song, every time:

There was once a *baby* koala so *soft* and *round*
that *a-l-l* who saw her *loved* her. Her *name* was
Ko-*ala* Lou.

The ups and downs of our voices and our pauses and points of emphasis are like music, literally, to the ears of young children, and kids love music. Simple tunes also make anything easier to remember, so it's useful to read a book in exactly the same way every time, and, as I've said earlier, to read the same book over and over again. The more quickly children pick up the tune of the words, the more they'll remember the words and the more quickly they'll have fun trying to "read" the story themselves, with the same expression as we use.

☆

Though it's true that there's no exact right way to do it, reading aloud is in fact an art form in which the eyes and voice play important parts. Here are a few hints about how to make the most of both, as well as some general advice on how to read all stories aloud in a more entertaining manner.

If we read a story without allowing its emotional value to show through our eyes, we're wasting a prime asset. Stanislavsky, the great Russian theater director, said the eyes are the windows of the soul. Unfortunately it's all too common for curtains to fall over those windows when we begin to read aloud. The story ought to be in the eyes as much as it's in the mouth. Animation in the eyes isn't difficult. We can widen them, narrow them, use them to "think" with, to be "shocked" with, to be "scared" with, to "listen" with, to be "happy" with, and so on.

Next, the voice. The great worry about focusing on the voice is that we might become falsely over-expressive. We don't want to go so far as to be absurd or embarrassing, but we must aim at least to be highly interesting. The one thing to avoid in reading aloud is a cutesy, sugary, patronizing voice. We have to make a conscious decision *never* to talk down to children.

Authors hope we'll carry out their intentions faithfully by letting their words instruct us, not the other way around. For instance, it would be crazy to shout: "Voices whispered in bushes." The word *whisper* tells us very clearly how to say it.

We can do at least seven things with our voices to keep our listeners engaged. Six of these seven vocal gymnastics are contrasts: loud and soft, fast and slow, and high and low. And we can p-a-u-s-e. The words on the page will tell us which of these to choose. We don't need speech training. We simply need to pay close attention. Obvious examples of these vocal in-flections are illustrated in the following excerpts from my own books.

Here's a soft-voice example from *Night Noises*, in which the family of a much-loved ninety-year-old has planned a surprise birthday party:

Somewhere in the distance car doors opened
and closed softly. CLICK. CLACK.... Feet tip-
toed up the garden path. CRINCH, CRUNCH....
Voices whispered in bushes. MURMUR,
MUTTER, SHHHH.

☆

Now an obvious loud-voice example, also from *Night
Noises:*

Fists beat upon doors and voices shouted at windows. YELL, CLATTER, BANG, BANG, BANG.

☆

A slow voice is best used for the darkest moments in
a book. Here's a slow-voice example from *Wombat Divine,* in which stagestruck Wombat has auditioned for
a part in the Nativity play, to no avail.

And then there were no parts left. Wombat
hung his head and hoped he wouldn't cry.

☆

A fast voice, needless to say, is for the speedier
parts of a text, or for any other section filled with

excitement and drama. This excerpt is from *Koala Lou* when she takes part in the all-important Bush Olympics, on which her highest hopes are pinned:

> Koala Lou leapt onto the tree. Up and up and up she climbed—higher and higher and higher. Faster and faster and faster until—there she was, right at the very top! The spectators roared and clapped and stamped their feet.

☆

The high voice, as with the fast voice, can also be used in moments of great excitement or drama. In *Hattie and the Fox,* when the identity of a scary animal in the bushes is finally revealed to the big black hen, she says:

> "Goodness gracious me! I can see a nose, two eyes, two ears, a body, four legs, and a tail in the bushes! It's a fox! It's a fox!" And she flew very quickly into a nearby tree.

☆

Low voices are terrific for frightening parts of a story or for voices that should be low, like the voices of pirates or giants. In *Wilfrid Gordon McDonald Partridge*, with its six elderly characters, we need to change our voice in order to differentiate between each one. Wilfrid visits one of his elderly friends, Mr. Drysdale, "who had a voice like a giant," and asks him what a memory is. Mr. Drysdale replies in a deep voice, obviously:

"Something as precious as gold, young man, something as precious as gold."

☆

The pause can be used to great effect before a dramatic mood change in the story or, indeed, if there is an obvious pause in a character's speech. In this excerpt from *Harriet, You'll Drive Me Wild!*, pesky little Harriet has been accident-prone all day. Through it all her mother has managed to keep her cool. Crunch time comes when Harriet and her dog accidentally rip open a pillow.

A thousand feathers flew in every direction. [Long pause] There was a terrible silence. [Long pause] Then Harriet's mother began to yell. [Pause] She yelled and yelled and yelled.

☆

At the Rose Bruford drama school in London in the sixties, I was taught how to read and tell stories by Rose Bruford herself, the most gifted storyteller I've ever heard. She, in turn, had been taught storytelling by the poets W. B. Yeats and John Masefield, who were anxious to revive storytelling as an art form in its own right.

Because she had worked with these master craftsmen, Miss Bruford had learned how to pay attention to the detail of every single individual word, whether she was telling a story or reading aloud. She created a world of enchantment by concentrating on loving the words and magically revealing the hidden meaning in each one—dead sentences came alive, seemingly unimportant words leapt off the page. We can do the same, if we allow the words in the stories we're reading aloud to communicate their nuances.

To illustrate the importance of apparently minor words, try replacing *jumped* with *crawled* or *clambered* in the following excerpt from *Sleepy Bears*:

> So the little bears jumped into the soft feather bed and pulled up the covers as fast as they could.

Clearly, *jumped* is tremendously important here because of the energy and speed it conveys, and we should do our best to "jump" with our voices, rather than "crawl" or "clamber," both of which are more reluctant than "jump."

Similarly, in *Koala Lou*, *filled* is of utmost importance and poignancy in this passage:

> She saw her mother in the crowd and imagined
> her saying again, "Koala Lou, I DO love you!"
> Her heart filled with hope.

The word *filled* is usually such an insignificant, common little word, we might well forget to use it to its fullest when we're reading aloud. But here the line is meant to convey so much meaning that the word *filled* needs to be colored in with a rising voice.

We need to notice these and other apparently humdrum individual words and relish them. What we love, our listeners will love. If children love the words they hear, they'll use them delightfully in their own speaking and in their own writing. If they love the sounds of the words, they'll understand them better when they come to read them later. That's another terrific benefit of reading aloud: familiar words—words heard often previously—are always easier to read than unfamiliar words.

☆

One of the easiest ways of attempting excellence when we're reading aloud is to really see, in our mind's eye, the things we're reading about. We need to *see* the brand-new visible tail in *Possum Magic*. *See* the blood-stained stillness in *Feathers and Fools*. *See* the spilled paint on the carpet in *Harriet*. *See* the progress of the characters through each book we read.

For example, in this sentence, taken from *Koala Lou*, "She...lifted weights and panted," the word *lifted* seems humdrum, even mundane. Yet if we *see* the scene and allow our voice to lift as we say it, if we allow our head to rise as we say it, if we feel the sensation of lifting and reflect that feeling in our eyes, then the word *lift* is truly communicated to our listeners.

☆

The way we speak the first line should be sensational. The aim is to grab our audience immediately and never let them go. Even the opening sentence from *Possum Magic*, "Once upon a time, but not very long ago, deep in the Australian bush lived two possums...," can be made fascinating by a long pause after "Once upon a time," then a quick, secretive look

around to see if it's safe to read the rest of the sentence, and then an emphasis on the words *deep* and *two*. All at once it comes alive.

Not only should the first line be a gathering together and a dynamic grabber of our audience, it should also be a sentence of welcome to the ritual of the read-aloud session. So, as we say the dynamic first line, we know we're also saying, through the words of the story: "Hello, hello! Welcome! It's divine to be here with you."

☆

Now to endings. If anything could be more important than the first line of a story, it's the last line. If our story reading is as mesmerizing as it should be, the last line will be akin to the final amen at the end of a church service and will provide this kind of reassurance to the child: "Good-bye for now, go well, God bless you, take it easy, you're safe with me, I love you very much, see you soon."

Badly read endings are the tragic ruin of many an excellent story. We need to be absolutely certain of the words we're going to read so we don't stumble over them. Here's the last line in *Feathers and Fools:*

So off they went together, in peace and unafraid, to face the day and share the world.

Whenever I read that line in a read-aloud workshop, with the participants joining in, I always finish last because I'm the only one who says the line slowly enough. Training ourselves always to d-r-a-g o-u-t t-h-a-t l-a-s-t l-i-n-e takes awhile, but the more slowly we say it, the more satisfied our listeners will be.

We can achieve great things emotionally if the last line is a definite dismissal, a farewell. As we say it, we're releasing our listeners from their contact with us. Without this drawn-out final line, our listeners will feel an uncomfortable sort of incompleteness. A rapid finish feels oddly wrong. A slow finish is an absolutely delicious experience. Both teller and listeners find themselves in a state of bliss, akin to "living happily ever after."

☆

When I was lecturing would-be teachers on how to teach reading and writing, there was so much material to cover, I was able to allocate only one pitiful hour in the whole course to the art of reading aloud. Yet I was surprised year after year by how well my students read aloud at the end of the semester. *How had they done it,* I wondered, *with so little training*? They'd learned it from listening to me reading aloud, which I did regularly and often. The mere example of my reading aloud had done the trick. They had picked it up through their ears.

Expressive reading is reading that is remembered. And so it is with our own children. They'll read with exactly the same expressive inflections as we do, which is why we should make the effort to read aloud with vitality and lots of vocal variation.

☆

It's hard to explain in written form how to do interesting things with voices when we're reading aloud, although that's been my intention in this chapter. If you have access to the Internet, it may be useful to listen to me reading this chapter aloud on my Web site. I also read three complete books on the same site. The address is www.memfox.net, and the section is called, not surprisingly, "Reading Aloud."

☆

CHAPTER SEVEN

Getting the Most Out of It

Finding a book, getting a child, and sitting down and reading the book to the child is *completely* fine on its own. It's exactly what we should be doing.

It is possible, however, to enrich and add value to a read-aloud session, thereby making it even more fun and of even greater benefit to our eager listeners, simply by playing games with the books we're reading. We don't need any special talents or knowledge to be able to provide a solid literacy grounding for our children. We don't need drills and skills, or horrible workbooks, or expensive programs. We should *not* suddenly become teachers of our children. We must be ourselves. Entertainment is the teacher. Subtlety is the key.

We absolutely must not attempt to teach our children formally before they start school. For parents to teach their own preschool children is the last straw. Teaching is the flip side of what works. Teaching before school kills the fun. Preschool children like their parents to be parents, not teachers. The roles are quite

different, and it's precisely the laid-back, hang-loose, let's-have-fun, relaxed-and-comfortable role of a parent that is so powerful in helping children first to love reading and then to be able to read by themselves.

But because we now know so much about the incredible agility of the brain and its need to feed on stimulation from the moment of birth, we might become tense about our reading-aloud responsibilities. What if we fail our kids by doing too little? What if we do the wrong thing? What if we expect too much? It's so daunting that it could have a freak-out effect on some parents, especially on families in which the sole parent or both parents are in the workforce. Hearts might sink. And the despondent parent might well protest: "I can't fit anything more into my stressed-out life. Am I supposed to teach my kids while I'm reading to them or not? What am I supposed to *do*?"

When Eamon was three years old and Allyn, my editor, was reading an early draft of this book, she certainly felt panic rising.

"What do you mean when you say enrich but don't teach?" she asked. "What are you supposed to do when you're reading aloud, then?"

"Act naturally," I said. "Don't do anything differently from what you'd normally be doing."

"Like, you mean, when I notice that *goose* and *loose* rhyme, I sort of say: 'Goose and *loose*...Hey, Eamon, that's a rhyme! *Goose* and *loose!*' And then I read on. That kind of thing? Because I guess I already do that."

"Exactly," I said.

☆

We need to remain upbeat and keep very calm as parents. We mustn't allow ourselves to be rattled. We have to be sensible. We won't really be altering what we're already doing, unless we're not yet reading aloud to our children, in which case we will, of course, hop to it immediately!

What we'll be doing is playing spontaneous reading games that will provide many happy experiences and make learning fun. I used to invent simple games on the hop, when the right moment presented itself—whenever Chloë said something I could pick up and run with. I encourage every parent to mess about in a similar fashion. The games we play with books are best when they are completely off-the-cuff, unplanned, unexpected, and unique to that one child at a precise moment. Imposing a set of ideas thought up by someone else isn't the aim. The examples included here are merely a guide to possibilities, not a prescription of exactly what should happen.

When Lyn Wilkinson, a close friend and colleague of mine, was young, her dad used to play a variety of games when he was reading aloud to her. He wasn't a teacher by profession, and he would have claimed to know nothing about the teaching of reading.

He was aware that Lyn knew how to hold a book and turn the pages correctly, so he'd tease her by deliberately starting to read from the last page. She'd say, "No, Daddy! You don't read it like *that*! You read it like *this*!" And she'd point him to the first page.

Sometimes he would turn the book upside down, and she'd react as if he were a complete idiot and turn it the right way up. He was certainly teaching, but he was teaching without teaching because it was a game.

Another silliness he engaged in was to get a book, like *Little Red Riding Hood,* and start to read: "Once upon a time, there were three little pigs..." Lyn, looking at the pictures and being familiar with both stories, would say: "No, Daddy, can't you *seeeeee*? This book's about Little Red Riding Hood, not the three little pigs!" Once again her father was making a valid teaching point—that the illustrations match the words in a picture book—merely by fooling around.

It's important to point out here the significance of the illustrations in books for young children. We mustn't skip over them. The pictures tell a thousand words and help unlock the action of the story. In some read-aloud sessions, we're not even reading at all—we're talking back and forth about the illustrations and what's in them. The younger the child, the more we'll be chatting together about the pictures, and it will be the child more often than not who'll start the discussion.

☆

It's crucial for us to continue to keep in mind, as Lyn's dad did, that we're not teaching when we're enriching a read-aloud experience. We're playing and having a good time. Pressure on the child is absolutely forbidden. We won't be allowing phrases such as "No, no! That's wrong! Don't be so silly!" to slip from our careless lips. Tension or anxiety should *never* interfere with the reading-learning equation. Losing the joy means losing the usefulness.

☆

To demonstrate more games we might play, I'll use a short book of mine: *Tough Boris*. Here's the complete text:

> Once upon a time, there lived a pirate named
>> Boris von der Borch.
>
> He was tough.
> All pirates are tough.
> He was massive.
> All pirates are massive.
> He was scruffy.
> All pirates are scruffy.
> He was greedy.
> All pirates are greedy.
> He was fearless.
> All pirates are fearless.
> He was scary.
> All pirates are scary.
> But when his parrot died, he cried and cried.
> All pirates cry.
> And so do I.

The first and most obvious activity to do with any book is to read it, and read it again, and read it once more, and then again and again. If it's a favorite book, it cannot be read aloud too often. Repetition is even better if our young listeners can see the text while we're reading aloud so their eyes can follow the words as our voice passes over them. A finger under the line isn't necessary. Again and again, the child will be able to see the same words spelled in the same way, the same punctuation, the same italics, the same capitals, the same bold print, and so on.

To encourage the eyes to look carefully at the print, here's a look-at-the-words game. At first we're doing all the talking:

> Parent points to the two words that say *tough* and exclaims:
>
> "Hey, this word's the same as that word! They both say *tough*. Amazing! I bet *all* the pages repeat words. Do they? How crazy!"
>
> Turn the page.
>
> "Yes! It says *massive* here, and look! Here's the same word here: *massive* again! I wonder what's on this page."
>
> Turn the page.
>
> "*Scruffy!* Look! This word says *scruffy*. Can we find it in another place as well? It starts with an *s* which looks like this..."
>
> Show the child the *s*.
>
> "Hey, you're right! *Scruffy!* Brilliant!"

And so on. It should remain a game. If our darlings can't find the word, we will find it for them and pretend they found it by themselves. And we'll hug them for trying so hard. Tension should never occur. All gains are lost when tension curdles the relationship.

Gradually, over several more nights of this and similar silly games made up on the spot, children will be able to identify all the words in the story that describe Boris: *tough, massive, greedy, scruffy, scary,* and so on.

☆

When we play games with books, we *always* begin with a whole real story that excites and engages the child, a story that will become familiar over many readings. Then, continuing our game playing, the child can look for individual words and read those words aloud. For example, after we've read *Tough Boris* again, we could say, "You know something? I think it says *He was* on just about every page of that book. Look, here it is on this page. And here it is on this page as well. I wonder if it's on the other pages. It starts with a capital *H* like this [point to it], and there are two separate words: *He* and *was*. Can we find them, or aren't they on every page after all? I could be wrong." The child will find them. *Brilliant child,* we think to ourselves.

"How exciting!" we say aloud.

We might go on to try to find all the common words on different pages of a story, such as *and* and *the* and *because,* remembering all the while that it isn't teaching. It's a noisy game, played in a spirit of fun.

Next we can play a game that will move the child even further along—to reading and sounding out individual letters.

☆

At this point, I must sidetrack for a very important moment to clarify the cheerful direction we're taking here along the road to reading. It may indeed seem back-to-front to *start* with whole stories, then to *advance* to whole words, and then to *advance* again to individual letters and their sounds. The popular view is that we should start the other way around and teach using a phonics-first approach. Phonics is making the right sounds out of letters and their combinations. Most parents assume (with some logic) that they should start with letters first, and then go on to words, and then to stories, but anyone truly familiar with the way children learn to read most easily and happily knows that the stories-to-words-to-letters method is far more effective.

While phonics is one element in learning to read, the stories-first approach to reading achieves better results than the letters-and-phonics-first approach. Stories-first takes care of the essential *attitude* problem. Children who have been endlessly entertained by wonderful stories have a joyful attitude toward learning to read.

In the so-called reading wars (in which people argue with deadly ferocity over the best way of teaching reading), some educators claim to be antiphonics. This is foolish. Knowing phonics is an important part of learning how to read. It is only a problem when the teaching of reading *starts* with phonics, or when the teaching of reading focuses on phonics alone to the exclusion of everything else.

☆

Having cleared up *that* thorny issue, we can now move into a reading-individual-letters game. Children usually know the names of the letters of the alphabet early on in their lives. But we need to remember that although they know the ABC song, many young children can't identify single letters when they see them in *print*. Being able to correctly identify the individual letters of the alphabet before school is a great predictor of a child's future success as a reader.

How can children learn to recognize individual letters in print? By us playing silly, spontaneous games with them to see if they can find, for example, a particular letter on a particular page of the story. We could say: "That's the letter *e*. Can you find all the *e*'s on this page? Then you choose a page for me and I'll find all the *e*'s on *that* page, and we can see who finds the most."

Or in *Tough Boris*, for example, it might be fun for a child called Mem to look for as many examples of the letter *m* as possible, and the parent could do the same. Let's say the parent's name is Tom. He could start the game as if surprised one day to see the letter *t* in the book.

"Hey, look: that's a *t*. I've got a *t* in my name. Let's see if we can find an *m* for you. And another. Yay! And another! *Yes!*"

☆

When I'm playing with letters, I nearly always call them by name—A, B, C—rather than by sound—*uh, buh, cuh*—because many letters have more than one sound. The letter *a* doesn't always sound like it does in *apple*. It has many different sounds in different words such as *tuba, terrace, chat, balmy, ache,* and *hare.* And the *c* in *cat* is different from the *c* in *gracious* and *church,* which is different again from the *ch* sound in *echo.* There are hundreds of confusing differences in the sounds of various letters and their combinations, but the names of the letters never change, which is why it's so safe to use them.

It is of course important for children to be able to identify the most basic sounds of the letters of the alphabet as well. This is best explored with simple words that are easy to sound out, such as *Hop on Pop* or *Do not run!* rather than with words like *New South Wales,* which are a phonics nightmare.

We can play games that explore turning print into sound by using fridge magnets, which provide a great way for kids to mess around with the alphabet. The letters can be moved from one day to the next to spell children's own names, as well as simple words like *mom* and *dad.*

And we might play a game by starting with a

word like *can* and changing one letter at a time (per day? per minute? who cares?) to make new words.

- Take away the *n* and put in a *t* and, hey presto, we have *cat!*

- Take away the *c* and put in an *r* and, hey presto, we have *rat!*

- Take away the *a* and put in a *u* and, hey presto, we have *rut*!

- Take away the *t* and put in a *b,* and, hey presto, we have *rub* . . . and so on.

If the child moves the letters to make the new words, it's even more fun.

☆

Fridge magnets didn't help one mother as fast as she had hoped, but she didn't get discouraged. She and I were standing in line at the bank chatting about literacy (what else!), and she told me about how quickly her daughter had learned her letters. The little girl could make her name with fridge magnets at the age of two and a half. Then this proud mother had a son. To her chagrin, he showed no interest at all in books, words, or letters.

Finally one day when he was three, he did take a sudden and intense interest in the fridge magnets: he opened the door of the freezer and tossed each one of them into it in a pretend game of basketball. Not to be outdone, his mother left them there, and from time to time she would yank a frozen magnet from the ice and say: "Tyler, here's your frozen *e*! And look, here's your frozen *j*. How about that?"

Still nothing happened. Then one day when she walked in from work, Tyler grabbed her by the arm and said, "Mama, look what I've done. I've written my name!" The fridge magnets that had been rescued from the freezer were all in a straight line in no particular order, right across the fridge. Something had finally clicked in Tyler's head: he'd realized that letters can make words—even though he hadn't written a "real" word—and he was on his way to reading.

☆

Another brilliant way for children to learn the sounds of the letters is to encourage them to try to write, even when it's only scribble. Amazing as it may seem, trying to write is one of the fastest ways children teach themselves to read.

When we allow children to work out the relationships between letters and their sounds by writing or trying to write, they very quickly learn the sounds of the letters and letter combinations they need. They ask a whole lot of questions at first and will need a lot of assistance, but if we encourage them to have a go and use their own brains first, before they pick ours, they will learn actively and quickly. They love to write. In fact, most young children think they *can* write, whereas, interestingly, they don't think they can read.

It's a great idea to keep piles of scrap paper, little notebooks, butcher's paper, and even newspaper around, so there's always something nearby for them to write on. A variety of writing implements also helps: fat crayons, thin crayons, lead pencils, colored pencils, and even markers and ballpoints if we're risk takers and don't care what happens to the furniture.

When children write, they'll sound out some of the letters and name others. For example, when they write the word *home,* they'll make the sound of the *h* and the *m* but put a name to the *o* and thus get the word and sound of *home* even though they'll only write *hom.* As they focus on half sounding and half naming the letters, they'll say to themselves: "*huh, oh, muh . . . home.*"

(This invented spelling is an excellent method of self-teaching the sounds of individual letters and should be wildly encouraged in the young learner but firmly discouraged in the older child. Sooner or later, perhaps by the age of eight, kids will have to realize that they're not expected to get spelling right simply because society says it's essential to get it right. They need to understand that they must get it right in order to convey their message clearly, without a fuss, without a hitch.)

☆

It's important for a child's feelings of self-worth to be able to "read" without really recognizing the individual words at first. After children have been exposed to wonderful whole *stories* and to the idea of whole *words* and separate *letters,* they can pretend to read a book. And because we have read aloud the book in question so often before, they will be able to freely and quickly join in and "read" words and phrases all by themselves. Any repetitive book makes this activity easy, and the success associated with it increases children's confidence and self-esteem. For example, using *Tough Boris* again, we could start like this:

> Parent: He was tough.
> Child: All pirates are tough.
> Parent: He was massive.
> Child: All pirates are massive . . . [and so on]

We could then ask them to "read" all of *Tough Boris* to us from memory by pretending we're too tired and letting them do it by themselves, making any old mistakes they like. They can pretend to decipher the words as if they *were* reading, with the same aplomb, the same tune, and in the same fluent manner as we have done.

When children have heard a book so often that they know it by heart and can fool us into thinking they're reading—they're turning the pages at the right time and saying the right words on the right page—we shouldn't be tempted to belittle their efforts by saying: "Well, of course they're only reading it off by heart."

Turning the pages at the right time and saying the right words on the right page is a *tremendous* achievement for little kids, and not to be underestimated. It's a giant step toward really reading. In fact, children who know books by heart find it much easier to correctly read those books in due course. It's as if they say to themselves: "All right, I know exactly what this story is about, and I know every single word in it, so now let me look at the print and find out which one of these words is which. This must be the one that says *invisible* because it starts with *in*, and I can read that. It's easy."

☆

We have an audiotape of Chloë at six reading *The Beast of Monsieur Racine* by Tomi Ungerer for her grandparents, all of whom lived overseas. It is a wonderfully wacky and wicked picture book with very tasty vocabulary, far too difficult for a young child to read fluently and often difficult to understand, but Chloë knew it almost by heart and insisted on choosing it for the tape recording. So she said *frockled* instead of *frolicked* and *akdamee of sinuses* instead of *Academy of Sciences*. (We still say *frockled* in our family—more of that connecting "togetherness" code that I mentioned in Chapter Three.) But in spite of these hiccups over the hard words, her reading of the story is surprisingly fluent.

Later, when I became a literacy consultant, I came across the tape of Chloë reading and was pulled up short by the lesson it taught me. It was Malcolm, not I, who recorded her reading the story. He knew nothing about teaching-of-reading dogma. He told her the words she didn't know, without hesitation, while she was reading, which meant she could get on with the story at a lickety-split pace.

Unlike the "ignorant" Malcolm, many teachers and well-meaning parents—including me—have told children to sound out a word they don't know, or to go back or read forward to see if they can figure out what the word might be. But because Malcolm *didn't* make Chloë sound out the words, her guessing—that is, her reading—was able to be more accurate. And she never lost interest in the story or felt she couldn't read it. The further along she got, the fewer words Malcolm had to help her with. Because she was going quickly, she was able to remember more easily what she'd just read in the story, which helped her read what was to come. She also used the print, of course, as all readers do. Her self-esteem soared.

Our habit of constantly reading aloud to Chloë meant that for her sounding out words was a very rare occurrence, no matter what the book. She used her memory of stories and a basic understanding of print and story language to make sense of it all. I can't remember her sounding out any words at all unless they were really complex. Chloë learned to read early because she rarely had to stop, go back, or sound out words, which meant reading for her was interesting, not tedious.

Isn't that what we want for all our children?

CHAPTER EIGHT

The Proof

☆

The Proof

A woman stopped me in the street a few years ago after I'd appeared on a national television program and said: "You're that read-aloud woman, aren't you?" Was that who I was? Who I'd become? I could think of worse names.

That night I received a message on my Web site from Allan Bartlett, a parent in Melbourne who also knew me from television as "that read-aloud woman." He and his wife, Donna, had read aloud regularly to their son with remarkable results. Justin was then twenty-one months old.

Justin had been introduced to books at six days old. It had seemed to his parents like a good thing to do—something a bit more interesting than just feeding him and changing his diapers—and he seemed to like books and being read to, right from the start.

From day to day and week to week, his enjoyment of books grew steadily. By three months he clearly knew which way a book should be held, and he could even turn the pages on cue, responding to the obvious pause in reading at the end of a page. By *three months*!

Before long he began to develop favorites, most of which had simple rhyming words or the fascination of moving pieces. By six months he could identify many of his books by pointing to the title on the cover, and he was becoming more and more aware of tracking the print from left to right. Twenty little books in a one-hour sitting didn't make him flinch.

He was soon able to say two or three words together on a regular basis. He also attempted to "read along" with his parents when they were reading to him and filled in the gaps they left out of certain sentences. He knew his books virtually by heart.

At twenty-one months this very young child had a speaking vocabulary in excess of five hundred words, which his mother attributed to what he had gained from books. He could also sight-read about twenty words.

This amazing information could send us into a compare-and-despair depression. But let's choose to be inspired, uplifted, and encouraged instead. After all, Justin's learning was coincidental. It had been fun. His parents didn't do anything super special with him, except love him, play with him, read to him, and provide him with plenty of books and the time to enjoy them.

Justin could be anyone's child: yours or mine, or the little kid next door. He isn't gifted. He isn't special. He's normal. But he does have an incredible blessing in his life: parents who read aloud to him.

CHAPTER NINE

☆

The First Secret of Reading: The Magic of Print

Most of us think we know what reading is, and that's not surprising. After all, we can read. But reading is tricky. Reading is complex. Reading isn't merely being able to pronounce the words correctly, a fact that surprises most people. Reading is being able to make *sense* from the marks on the page. Reading is being able to make the print *mean* something. Reading is getting the message.

There is a bag of tricks we all use when we read, whether we realize it or not—no matter what age we are or what language we speak—and in it are three secrets that help us to get the message.

☆

The first secret of reading is hardly a secret. It's the ability to recognize and make sense of the many little squiggles on a page. For example, none of us can the read the following, #@◉★⊚🌙*∫√ π^Å°¿Æ/◉ 🌙*∫ ‡!¨≈ ◊ø 🌙*∫√Δ‹Ω🌙*∫√^ ⊚√ π^Å°#@*∫ ‡!¨≈, because we can't make sense of the symbols, no matter which way we look at it. It means nothing to us. Similarly, those of us who know only English are unable to get anything meaningful from a Russian edition of the Old Testament or from Hebrew instructions for a digital camera because we aren't able to make heads or tails, literally, out of what's on the page. To get the message, we must be able to recognize and understand the print symbols and their various combinations. So, if we want our children to learn how to read anything—let alone to read more, or to read more diverse or more difficult material—it helps immeasurably if we can give them as much experience of print as possible.

☆

We can imprint print by reading aloud to children— even babies (especially to babies, as I've said often before and will say again). As they're looking at the book and watching the pages turn, they will see the print and hear its meaning. The more they see of the printed word, the more they will understand its peculiarities— such as the letter combinations *tch, sh, th, ight,* and words ending in *tion.* Eventually the peculiarities will become so familiar to the child's eye, they won't seem peculiar anymore. Children will also begin to understand that getting the message from print means being able to recognize the shapes of entire words, the look of capital letters, punctuation, bold print, italics, headlines, columns, tables of contents, and so on.

Print isn't found only in books. It's everywhere in towns and cities and is a surprisingly efficient resource for helping children learn to read. The more we read aloud together with them any print we can see at the same time—such as signs, billboards, notices, posters, and license plates—the better. Car, train, and bus rides provide a million opportunities for print spotting, many of which can be turned into games we can make up on the spur of the moment as we go along, such as "Who can find the most stop signs in the next ten minutes?" Or "Who'll be first to see a capital *R*?"

By two, Chloë was able to read the signs of all the gas stations in our town: Shell, BP, Mobil, Ampol, and so on, as well as the words she saw most often on street signs, such as STOP, and TURN LEFT ANY TIME WITH CARE, merely from our calling them out as a game on car journeys.

Another two-year-old child in my acquaintance used to see the advertisement for the Commonwealth Bank on the backs of buses so frequently that eventually he asked his parents what it said. After that, he would read it aloud whenever it appeared on a bus. At first his mother thought he was merely recognizing the familiar logo of the bank. Then one day when her husband was reading the newspaper in which there was a headline about a meeting of the Commonwealth Heads of Government, the child pointed to the word *commonwealth* and said: "That says *commonwealth.*"

Brilliance off the back of a bus! Yet most people would seriously doubt that a two-year-old could read a perplexing word like *commonwealth.* (He certainly didn't sound it out.)

☆

When so-called experts shortsightedly extol a phonics-only approach to learning reading, I remind them of the fact that only 50 percent of English words are spelled the way they sound phonically. So what do we do about the other 50 percent? Ignore them? The craziness of English spelling knows no bounds, which is one of the great weaknesses of phonics. Meaning can't always come from turning print into sound. Take the word *nice,* for instance. Focusing on sounding it out phonically—*nuh-ih-kuh-eh*—is wildly inefficient and gets us precisely nowhere. It's much easier to read *nice* correctly when it's surrounded by a scaffold that helps us make a good guess, such as the rhyme "Sugar and spice, and all things *nice.*"

And how can phonics help in situations when we're faced with the following words that look similar but are all pronounced differently: *cough, enough, bough, through,* and *though*? Phonics is important, certainly, but it isn't "enuff" on its own. (Of course, when we're reading aloud, we definitely need to be able to turn print into sound—especially, and obviously, when we come to a difficult word we've never met before, no matter what the letter combinations are.)

If we were Italian, phonics would be more useful, most of the time: *Ti amo, cara* is much easier to sound out correctly than *I love you, darling*, since it's hard for children to guess that the phonics of *love* is *luv*. Beginning readers might well expect *love* to sound out as *lovvy*, or for it to rhyme with *drove* or perhaps with *move*.

☆

There are times when readers—young and old—can see the print and read it phonically yet can't decipher it enough to make meaning out of it. Obviously, in such cases we can't read. Print will help English-only speakers to "read" certain languages like Spanish, Italian, and Indonesian because they are more or less written phonically. We can make the correct sounds out of the print, even though our pronunciation might be a little haywire. But we have to remind ourselves over and over again that reading means the ability to make *sense* out of the print, not *sound* out of the print. For example, this chorus from the Bahasa Indonesian edition of my book *Hattie and the Fox* can be easily "read" phonically by English speakers like you and me:

"Aduh, aduh!" kata angsa.
"Ya, ya, ya!" kata babi.
"Peduli apa?" kata domba.
"Birkan?" kata kuda.
"Apa lagi?" kata lembu.

But matching letters to the Indonesian sounds in the above *Hattie* chorus doesn't give English-speaking readers the essential element of sense. We aren't making any meaning out of the print we're reading, no matter how good our pronunciation. What we need and don't have here is an understanding of Bahasa Indonesian. We have to understand the language and how it works in order to be able to make sense of what we read. Print is not enough.

Which brings us to the second secret of reading...

CHAPTER TEN

☆

The Second Secret of Reading: The Magic of Language

Si on veut lire une langue, il faut d'abord comprendre la langue, is French for: If one wants to read a language, it is necessary first to understand the language. The more we know about a language—in our case, the more we know about how English works—and the more of that language we know, the easier it is to read it.

We can't read well without understanding the meaning of words, without understanding the clever ways words link to form sentences, without understanding how those words and sentences turn themselves into anything from books, paragraphs, and sentences, to shopping lists, Valentine's cards, magazines, advertisements, sports pages, and Web sites.

If we want our children to learn how to read any-thing—let alone to read more, or to read more diverse or more difficult material—it helps immeasurably if we can give them as much experience of language as possible.

☆

We can increase children's language experiences by chatting away to them as if they were our equals: by comforting a crying baby with soothing adult words; by discussing anything that's going on, no matter what age our children are, whether it be while we're changing diapers, shopping for bananas, discussing the likely end-of-season football results, arguing the pros and cons of marriage, or raving about the in-equities of globalization. Or by singing.

Songs and rhymes provide comforting rhythms in children's early lives and also expose kids to gorgeous forms of language. They are a natural extension to the heartbeat of the mother and the rhythmic rocking of a child in loving arms or in a cradle. They can be read, recited, chanted, or sung in a soft, low voice whenever a child is sleepy or fretful. And they're also fun to say and learn when children are wide awake and happy.

From songs, children learn words, sentences, rhythm, rhyme, and repetition, all of which they'll find later in the books they read. Kids who can't recognize the fact that two words such as *bed* and *Fred* rhyme—and there are many such kids—have a hard time learning to read, whereas those who *can* rhyme are able to make more inspired and more correct guesses about what a particular word might be when they are reading.

For example, in "Mary Had a Little Lamb," a child familiar with the rhyme would have no difficulty in reading the last word *go* because it so obviously rhymes with *snow:*

Mary had a little lamb
Its fleece was white as *snow,*
And everywhere that Mary went,
The lamb was sure to *go.*

Rhymers will be readers: it's that simple. Experts in literacy and child development have discovered that if children know eight nursery rhymes by heart by the time they're four years old, they're usually among the best readers by the time they're eight. I didn't know about the importance of songs and rhymes when Chloë was little, but as it happens, I used to sing to her every night as she was dropping off to sleep—songs, lullabies, spirituals, and nursery rhymes. Singing isn't for everyone, but the benefits are many, and, anyway, who's going to hear us? Only a child who loves us.

☆

The importance of getting songs and rhymes into children's heads can't be overestimated. This sounds easy enough to achieve, but it's surprising and depressing to discover how many children come to school these days without even the most basic rhymes in their heads.

A few years ago, when I was working with young schoolchildren for a television program about early literacy, things became very boring for the kids who were involved. Human error and technical hitches meant we often had to film a sequence two or three times. A six-year-old girl and I were commiserating with each other about how tedious it all was, and I suggested we say rhymes to pass the time.

"OK," she said, cheering up.

So I started with "Humpty Dumpty," but she

didn't know it and couldn't join in, although she seemed to enjoy it nevertheless. Next I tried "Mary Had a Little Lamb," but she didn't know that one, either. As I went through "Jack and Jill," "Hickory, Dickory, Dock," and "Baa, Baa, Black Sheep," it became clear she knew none of them.

"It's your turn now," I said. "You do one. I'm tired."

But she couldn't. At six she knew no rhymes at all! I felt so dismayed about her future, I almost broke my own rule and started to panic. Then I got hold of myself, kept calm, and set about teaching her "Three Blind Mice," which she giggled over but took awhile to learn because she wasn't in the habit of rhyming. Or singing, for that matter. And it's unlikely that she had ever enjoyed a poem, either.

After songs and nursery rhymes, poems are a logical next step. No one can resist old favorites like "Custard the Dragon" by Ogden Nash, or "The Highwayman" by Alfred Noyes, and "The Pied Piper of Hamelin" by Robert Browning, all of which can be found in the Louis Untermeyer classic, *The Golden Books Family Treasury of Poetry*, still in print after all these years.

horacek

Many people think children will dislike poetry, but that's far from the truth. Poetry only gets a bad name from adults whose opinions are colored by horrible high school memories of having to pick apart incomprehensible poems. Children get a real kick out of the bounce and wackiness of poetry, and poems can often be paths to literacy for children who have previously found reading difficult. A sixth grader I heard about in California finally cracked the code of reading when he was given a book of poems by Douglas Florian called *Bing Bang Boing*. The rhythmic rhyme and repetition in these hilarious poems clicked a switch in his head, and all of a sudden he was able to make sense of print. In other words, he learned to read.

And we mustn't forget the endearing poetic madness of the Dr. Seuss books with their inspired emphasis on rhythm, rhyme, and repetition. Chloë and I still know *Green Eggs and Ham* almost by heart from the heaps of times we read it together, even though we haven't done so for twenty-five years.

Once children have masses of rhythmic gems like these in their heads, they'll have a huge store of information to bring to the task of learning to read, a nice fat bank of language: words, phrases, structures, and grammar. The words in their heads then begin to drift into their daily speech, and all at once we have an articulate child.

☆

We should never underestimate what children can handle as readers and listeners. A teacher I know recently read *Les Misérables* to her sixth-grade class over an entire school year. No one suggested it might be unsuitable reading material for eleven-year-olds.

They loved the drama, the emotion, the action, and the love story, and they were agog every day as she read it. Anyone who was absent was frantic to find out what they had missed.

My doctor's grandson read all the Harry Potter books—one of which has over five hundred pages—by himself, avidly, at the age of six, along with millions of other children around the world. Who would have thought that possible?

Ellen, a teacher in Tennessee, read all the original poems from the musical *Cats* (which come from *Old Possum's Book of Practical Cats* by T. S. Eliot) to her son when he was three. He knew these poems by heart by the time he was four and a half because they'd been read to him, at his request, over and over and over again.

I must admit, this read-aloud story did surprise me. The vocabulary in Eliot's poems is highly sophisticated and the language so subtle, I'd have thought they would be too hard for such a young child to appreciate. I was aiming for the mud again in my thinking, like so many adults, instead of remembering to acknowledge the starry heights of children's abilities and potential.

On the other side of the coin, occasionally we do make mistakes about what children can cope with at a particular age. Dave, my editor's husband, was reading one of Rudyard Kipling's *Just So Stories* to his son, who had just turned four.

"Don't read that, Daddy," said Eamon. "It's too parent-ish."

Children are quick to tell us if they're bored. They'll put us straight very quickly if they think we've made the wrong choice. Each child is an individual, and preferences are often surprising. (Some four-year-olds might love the quaint nineteenth-century language in the *Just So Stories*.) But if as adults we're cool toward a particular book—if our literary and emotional temperature hasn't been raised, and if the children we're reading to aren't particularly rapt, either—we ought to put it aside. Enthusiasm from all quarters has to bubble around a book, or children will think reading is dull.

☆

As I've said, it's important, especially with younger children, to repeat the same lively stories over and over again, so book language loses its strangeness and becomes familiar. The language of books sounds different. It looks different. It *is* different.

For example, children who have little knowledge of the foibles of the English language would find it difficult to read this excerpt from the thrilling illustrated children's mystery *The Wedding Ghost* by Leon Garfield, especially the literary phrases and words in italics:

> Chains leaped from their fastenings, and lights came raining down from the dim ceiling, like *flights of stars*; and *the very walls* began to shake. . . . The congregation rushed *hither and thither,* shrieking and screaming; but their voices were drowned under the organ's *ceaseless* roar.

Children who have heard a lot of literary language read aloud will have little or no problem understanding this passage.

☆

Beginning readers also need to know that the language in sentences usually makes sense. Here's an example:

> Jack and Jill went up the hill
> To fetch a pail of sitting . . .

We'd be shocked if we read *To fetch a pail of sitting* in a nursery rhyme book. It would confound all the guesses we'd normally make as readers. *To fetch a pail of sitting* doesn't make sense in a sentence. We'd guess *water* because we expect language to make sense—after all, pails usually have water in them—and because we've heard the rhyme so often. We predict sense, because we know that's how language usually works. And knowing how language—in our case, English—works means we can read successfully.

☆

Children who haven't been read to don't expect print to make sense. And if children don't expect sense, they'll find learning to read very difficult. When they try to read for themselves, they'll often read *non-*sense because they've never experienced the sense in written language—the sense of rhyming, the sense of stories, the sense of songs, the sounds of unusual words, the unfamiliar formal grammar of written sentences, and the way sentences work.

Children who *have* been read aloud to regularly do expect to make sense from print. They know about rhyme and rhythm and repetition. They know how

real stories work, which makes it easier for them to read real stories. They can predict that certain words, patterns, and plots will occur, and they're proven right.

Yet some of the most badly written books in the world, commonly called "school readers"—and found,

of course, only in schools—are given to children who are learning to read! In the vacuous stories that fill these books, nothing of importance ever happens to anyone. Their dull stories make learning to read an uninspiring and dreary activity, and their crazy use of grammar confuses children's guessing, time and time again: "See Jip run. Run, Jip, run. Jip runs to the tree. See John. Run, John, run. See the tree," and so on. Where's the sense in this? We don't talk this way. No one talks this way.

But most dangerous of all, school readers send the message that reading is boring—so kids stop reading. And when they stop reading, they stop learning to read. And then we wonder why we have a literacy problem.

☆

If we understand English and how it works and if we also understand print, is it possible to read English correctly out loud but still not be "reading"? Yes, it is.

I was listening recently to a child reading a book that was too difficult for her to understand, though she could decipher and say the printed words. She ignored all the commas and periods and read each word with the same intonation. She was definitely sounding things out correctly, but she wasn't reading, although her mother thought she was indeed reading and was impressed.

"Can you tell me what the story's about?" I interrupted, pretending I was puzzled. "I've kind of lost track of it. What's been happening?"

She couldn't tell me. She hadn't understood the story because she wasn't using her knowledge of English. She was using phonics. She was reading in a way described by the experts as "barking" at print: saying each word correctly but without expression or meaning. So it is possible to read print correctly and also understand the language—yet not be reading.

☆

If knowing as much language as possible is the second secret of reading, what's the third secret?

CHAPTER ELEVEN

☆

The Third Secret of Reading: The Magic of General Knowledge

The third secret of reading is our general knowledge: all the stuff in our heads, gathered from birth to the present moment. The more we know about life, the universe, and everything, the easier it is to read.

For example, it's easy for a taxi driver who's crazy about golf and knows the meaning of words like *bogey* and *birdie* and *par* and *putt* to read and understand a detailed news report about golf. On the other hand, a cardiologist who knows absolutely nothing about golf might find such a report puzzling and difficult to understand. Yet a cardiologist who knows all there is to know about heart disease would easily be able to read and understand the writings of other cardiologists on the subject. The taxi driver would most likely find such information incomprehensible.

If we want our children to learn how to read anything—let alone to read more, or to read more diverse or more difficult material—it helps immeasurably if we can give them as much experience of the world as possible, in the same way that we provide as much experience as possible of the other two secrets of reading: understanding print and understanding language.

☆

We can provide a great deal of information by the act of reading itself. The more we read aloud to our kids and the more they read by themselves, the more experience they'll have of the world through the things they encounter in books. And the more experience they have of the world, the easier it will be to read.

When we read aloud to young children, they gain a vast amount of general knowledge, especially when they listen to stories they're unable to read by themselves. For example, in the classic children's picture book *Harry the Dirty Dog* by Gene Zion, this sentence appears: "He slid down a coal chute and got the dirtiest of all." This would be more difficult for children to read today than it was for children in 1956, when the book was first published. In 1956 many children would have understood what a coal chute was. They would have been able to read that phrase with comparative ease. Nowadays that sentence is more difficult for children to decipher because coal chutes are no longer part of their known world.

However, if we were to read *Harry the Dirty Dog* repeatedly to a child, talking about the pictures, laughing about the dog sliding in the coal at the bottom of the coal chute, and rejoicing in his return home, the idea of a coal chute would quite naturally become part of the child's known world. Afterward, when the child came to read the book by herself or himself, *coal chute* would present little difficulty.

☆

Of course children will not only learn about the world from the pages of books. They'll learn about it from being in it. It's important for us to take them on as many excursions as possible, even if it's just around the block to the local shops or to the park or the zoo, let alone to another state or country. They'll also gather information about the world by listening to interesting adults, watching fascinating television, and learning about anything at all—from computer graphics to making pancakes, milking a cow, or playing soccer. Expanding their experience in any direction helps them to better understand how the world works.

☆

Even we adults, with our huge knowledge of language and print, must have a certain level of knowledge of the world before we can easily read specific pieces of writing. Although you and I can actually "read" most English texts competently and correctly, are we really reading if the content happens to be way beyond our own understanding?

For instance, we may be able to "read" the following paragraph easily, but my guess is that only those who are passionate about postmodernism will be able to understand it:

> The continued existence of art as a coherent concept serves to protect the semiological discourse from the difficult problematic posed by the aesthetic.... The semiological inability to deal with this aesthetic is paradoxically ... due to its reliance on the preservation of the value-determined subcategory of art.

If we'd been tested on our reading skills by having to read that passage aloud, and if we'd made the right sounds, as indeed we would have, and if we'd paused in the right places, as indeed we would have because we understand how the English language works, any-one listening to us would have thought we'd under-stood the meaning of it. Yet the majority of us wouldn't have made much sense of it—even though we were able to use what we know about print and language—because we didn't have knowledge of that "world." As we spoke the words, we weren't saying something we could really understand, so we weren't "reading."

For this reason, it's crazy to try to assess chil-dren's reading abilities by simply asking them to read aloud. They might do it successfully yet have no un-derstanding of the text at all, and that's not reading! We need to chat with them about what they're read-ing to ensure they comprehend what's happening in the story, to find out if they're in the "world" of the story, to discover if they're really reading or not.

☆

We now know that reading comprises three clearly defined and separate "secrets": understanding print,

...bo...
...pa...
...the mill...
...to come do...
...he said. 'I've gr...
...now I'm off hom...
...s all over the village.
...e went very quiet, for i...
...g time, and he'd thought...
...nd about needing a man to p...
...it seemed as though he was wr...
...me he happened to pass near the...
...ved. There he heard something that...
...– it was the voice of the lass screaming...
...ust be a band of robbers that are after he...
...he set off at a run towards the lass's house.
...got there he found the door standing wide...
...s standing on the table, screaming loud enoug...
...And there at her feet was a wee brown mouse.
...ught you were the lass who was afraid of nothing,...
...lass opened her eyes and stopped screeching. 'Och, H...
...of that beastie for me. The cat's in the fields and the d...

understanding language, and understanding how the world works. When the three secrets of reading *combine*, the excitement really begins.

☆

What Happens When the Three Secrets of Reading Come Together?

When an understanding of the world, language, and print act together as a team, reading happens. All three go hand in hand, like inseparable friends. One assists the others. On their own they function badly. Reading is a grand guessing game, and if one of the secrets of reading fails to help us "guess" or read correctly, the other two kick in to help us along.

When children don't learn to read, or loathe reading, it's often due to too great a focus on one of the secrets of reading to the exclusion of the others. Many parents and teachers tend to focus too heavily on print for instance, not realizing the existence of the other two secrets and their importance.

When problems in reading occur, it's often effective to ask the child to use what she knows about the world and about "book" language to guess what a word might be. It might also be wise to stop having the child read aloud altogether and instead to read to her and play the games I talked about in Chapter Seven so she can experience even more of the very real pleasures of books.

☆

When we read, we take in as much information as we can as quickly as possible to help us predict more efficiently what the next word will be, and the one after that, and the one after that. We predict what's coming by making use of the print we see on the page, the language we understand, and the world that we know about. We predict and confirm at an astonishing rate.

For instance, if someone with careless handwriting sends us a postcard that says: "Had a great time house riding!" we may not be able to decipher the print, but our general knowledge tells us it has to be *horse* riding. We easily guess the right word, *horse,* and read the postcard correctly, because we know that people don't typically ride *houses.*

We read what we expect to read. In one of English cartoonist Graham Rawles's *Lost Consonants* cartoons, he has a mad picture of Shakespeare cooking, with the caption: "The collected woks of Shakespeare." It took me forever to notice the joke. As a product of drama school, I had such strong predictions about that sentence, based on what I know about the English language, theater, and Shakespeare's collected works, I couldn't see that the *r* had been left out of *works*, no matter how hard I looked.

☆

Those of us who are good readers of English don't have to understand or know how to pronounce every word we read. In this sentence, "It's difficult to read the beginning of Dostoyevsky's novel *The Brothers Karamazov* because of all its discombobulating Russian names," we may not fully understand the word *discombobulating*, but we know how English works, so we can guess from its position in the sentence that it means something like *confusing* or *unsettling*.

☆

The more we have read of any book, the more accurately we can guess what's to come. When we have read the same words, sentences, and stories many times before, there's a strong scaffold around the words on the page that helps us make excellent guesses as to their meaning.

As we read, we don't actually have to see every word. We don't need to. Many of them are unimportant. We skim, knowing in advance what many of the words are. When the unimportant words are left out, we can still make sense of a piece of writing if we read it quickly. For example, readers of this book will be able to read the following very quickly:

> The more we've...of any book...easier it...to read...rest of it because guessing...words becomes more and...accurate. We don't even have...read every word because so many... them are unimportant. We skim, knowing... advance what many of the words...be.

In our fast guessing, we make use of what we've just read. We use that immediate previous information to predict rapidly what's coming next. That's why when we're reading a difficult article or book, we can't seem to move on until we've pinned down the beginning and made it clear to ourselves. Once we've understood enough to move ahead and we've gathered sufficient information on which to base our guesses so we can make them accurate, we will be able to *read*.

For instance, many of us find it difficult to read the beginnings of Charles Dickens's novels because so many of the complexities of the plot are set up in the early pages and so many interconnecting characters are introduced. There are so few unimportant words, that we almost have to mouth each one as we read. We can't skim. We have to go back to the beginning again and again. Then based on that beginning— when we've finally understood it—we can predict and confirm much more quickly. The names and rela- tionships fall easily into place, and all at once we're skimming efficiently, racing ahead, wanting to know what happens next.

☆

To give them confidence, beginning readers need to be able to skim right from the start, which sounds like a contradiction: how can they skim if they can't read? Rhymes and songs provide many words that are easy to "read" since children know in advance—by the predictable rhyme and rhythm—what the correct word will be at the end of a given sentence. They don't have to "read-see" it. They can "read-guess" it. They begin to think of themselves as readers—the at- titude comes first, and the skills follow. Rhythmic, rhyming, repetitive stories give them instant "skimming" success in their early encounters with books and build their confidence.

In my book *Time for Bed*, for instance, there are many easy-to-guess words. Once children have heard the first two or three pages, they get the idea behind the pattern and "read" along, even if they can't see the book:

> It's time for bed, little mouse, little mouse,
> Darkness is falling all over the . . .
> It's time for . . . little goose, little goose,
> The stars are out and on the loose.
> It's time for bed, little cat, . . . cat,
> So snuggle in tight, that's right, like . . .

They quickly understand (as three-year-old Ben did, on the television program) that every page begins with: "It's time for bed. . . ." They know each animal is mentioned twice: ". . . little mouse, little mouse." They know every second line rhymes with the line before it: "It's time for bed, little cat, little cat / So snuggle in tight, that's right, like that."

In the end, children who are familiar with this type of bedtime rhyme understand so many of the words that they're able to make excellent guesses and can "read" it without looking. This is an important first step in reading development. From this point they will eventually and enthusiastically learn how to grapple with the print itself and learn how to truly read, using all three "secrets" of reading, including the print.

☆

Books like *Time for Bed* may give the impression that young readers don't actually need to see the print at all in order to be able to say the words correctly, but of course they do. They can make certain crucial guesses based very sensibly on their understanding of English and their general knowledge about the world—we all do—but seeing and understanding the print definitely makes correct guessing easier. We can't read accurately without it.

☆

The faster we read, the easier it is to read because we can hold in our memory all we've read so far, and then use that information to guess what's to come. Our memory clogs up quickly when we read slowly. We struggle word by word, and by the time we've worked out one word, we've forgotten what we have already read, so we can't use that information to help make sense of what we're about to read. It's a night-mare of confusion.

That's why it's harder to read aloud than it is to read silently, especially when we are reading unfamiliar material such as that earlier passage on postmodernism. The slowness of our progress overloads our memory and blocks out meaning. Yet over and over again in our folly, we ask the very readers who are struggling, the ones who read poorly, to read *aloud* to us! It's madness, and shows a deep lack of understanding of the reading process. What these kids need desperately is for us to read to them more often, and then for them to chat with us about what they've understood and enjoyed.

When young children agonizingly read an unfamiliar text out loud such as "The...thin...dog... growled...and...bared...his...teeth," they take so long to guess each word, they forget what they've already read in the story, and their brains shut down in fear, confusion, and boredom. All their previous information about the world, the English language, and print flies out the window.

Making print into sound becomes their only way of working out the meaning, which is woefully inefficient. Print is of minimal use until we add our understanding of the weird way words work in full sentences, especially when there are several possible meanings, such as in these examples:

> Yasser Arafat hurried home from France to deal
> with the building crisis.

Is that a crisis in the building industry? Or is a crisis building in intensity? How can we know, without reading the sentences before this one, or after it?

> Permit me to help you.
> They gave her the permit.

The meaning of *permit* depends on whether the first syllable or the second syllable of the word is emphasized, and we don't know which it will be until the word appears in a sentence.

> She wiped the tear off his cheek.
> He mended the tear in his shirt.

Once again, we know how to pronounce *tear* only by reading the other words in the sentence: one is pronounced *tier* and the other *tare*.

> The book was red.
> The book was read by the whole group.
> "Let's read it again!" they said.

In the first two sentences, *red* and *read* sound exactly the same. In the last two sentences, *read* and *read* are spelled the same yet sound totally different. We need the words surrounding each mystery word in order to decide which they are, and what they mean.

☆

We expect words to appear in sentences. It's rare in real life to have them separated from each other in random lists where there's nothing around them on which to base efficient guesses. (Most single words usually have no meaning on their own, although GO, STOP, and EXIT are obvious examples of exceptions.) Nothing makes sense in a list of unconnected words, yet children are often given these sorts of lists to "sound out":

> school
> bite
> then
> eager
> center
> admit
> shirk

It's more difficult for anyone—let alone confused children who are learning to read—to read lists of random words than to read those same words in normal sentences. It's misguided to ask children to identify lists of random unconnected words. It's even worse to ask children to pronounce words that have been completely made up and have no meaning at all, like *trom* or *feg*, as a way of trying to find out if they can read. It proves nothing about the totality of truly being able to read because only *one* of the three reading secrets is being employed: the print—and turning that print into sound.

☆

Good readers rarely have to sound out words, even though that might seem strange. You'd think they would be "good" at it, because they're good readers. Instead, good readers use the other secrets of reading—their general knowledge and what they know about language—to help them get the word right. Only then do they check the print to make sure their guess is correct. In fact, good readers use the *three* secrets of reading simultaneously, rapidly, and efficiently.

Poor readers use only one—phonics—and even that they use slowly. Sounding out words is the only way they know of making any sense out of the stuff on the page in front of them. Alas, sounding out may make them even poorer readers by boring them to sobs and frustrating the life out of them. (But let's remember that it is indeed hard for children—and for us—to read truly unfamiliar words if we can't sound out at least a few of the letters.)

When children are struggling to read one word at a time, we need to remember that for them it's like reading down a cardboard tube, or even a straw. They see only one or two words at a time. This stops them from reading correctly because they're reading too slowly to make sense. If we were to try reading down a straw ourselves, we'd see that we are barely able to make meaning from the page we're looking at. If it's difficult for us, imagine how much harder it must be for beginning readers to make any sense of what they're trying to read!

If we happen to be listening to a child who is struggling to read aloud and getting nowhere, we should stop the child, go back to the beginning of the story (tactfully), and read a few pages aloud ourselves. This will provide enough information for the child to get a grip on the plot. At the very least, it will clarify the names of the main characters, such as in a book like Judith Viorst's *Alexander and the Terrible, Horrible, No Good, Very Bad Day*. When the child has heard this story a few times, the name *Alexander* shouldn't be difficult to read. Then we can say: "All right, let's take turns. I'll start, then you read the next bit, and I'll read the bit after that."

☆

Astonishing and "soft" though this may seem, we should tell children the words they don't know, as Malcolm did when Chloë was reading *The Beast of Monsieur Racine* on tape. We need to hurry them along so their memory isn't overloaded, so they can use all the information they've picked up so far in the story (as well as use their understanding of the world, language, and print), to get accurate meaning as they read. Anything that slows them down is a bad thing. As I've said numerous times, they need to use the three secrets at the same time—print *and* language *and* general knowledge—in order to be able to read more easily. But children who are having difficulty are usually too tense to use the second two secrets, so they often fail to learn how to read, which means they often fail in their other subjects as well. All too soon they're viewed as "reading disabled."

To avoid this, we need to help beginning readers make rapid progress through a story so they're able to remember what they're reading. They'll then relax and make more sense of the print and eventually begin to enjoy the story. They will rely less on the single avenue of painfully sounding out words and will make informed guesses faster. Finally, they'll be reading. Eureka! And perhaps for the first time in their lives, they will realize that reading has fabulous, real rewards.

☆

At last we know what reading is! Without such information, we might find ourselves hanging on to outdated beliefs about reading that are just as odd and foolish as Jack and Jill going up the hill to fetch a pail of *sitting*.

By now we also know that it's much more effective in terms of reading development to read marvelous literature aloud to struggling readers than to ask them to read to us. If we read aloud a lot to children, the same stories repeated over and over, they learn to read quickly. The more familiar children are with a good book or story, the more easily they will be able to read it later, all by their clever selves.

Sad and shocking though it is, the incalculable benefits of reading aloud are not widely recognized or sufficiently promoted. Even when the benefits are known, many parents don't take them seriously enough because they feel that reading aloud is too simple and obvious to be that important.

"Oh, yeah," they say. "Reading aloud? Fine! I'll do that."

And they read a book aloud from time to time, but not often enough or regularly enough.

So let's help kids learn to read by reading aloud to them often, whenever we can, to make familiar what was once unfamiliar. Then let's read aloud again. And after that? Well, we'll read aloud! And all the while, we'll being playing those teaching-without-teaching, fooling-around, being-silly *games*.

CHAPTER THIRTEEN

☆

"Book! Book! Book!"

A librarian I know was out one day with a young father, helping him shop for birthday presents for his
daughter, who was about to turn five. "Why not buy
her a couple of books?" she asked.

"Books?" said the father. "Why would I buy her
books when she can't read?"

☆

The sister-in-law of a friend of mine was understand-
ably anxious when her children weren't picking up
reading skills as quickly as she had hoped. It turned
out that she had very few books in her house. They
"held too much dust"!

☆

A woman I know sent several picture books to her great-nephew for his second birthday. The mother of the child wrote back: "Thank you. What a neat idea!"

☆

Too many homes have no books in them. How can books become attractive if there aren't any lying around to flick through or to become absorbed in? There are highly privileged children in our society who can't read or won't read. It's not difficult to find out why. They have television and all the other commercial trappings of a well-off childhood, but they don't have books, so they never learn to love reading.

We shouldn't expect children to learn to read easily unless they have books in the house. Without books, where will kids see the print they need to see? When will they hear the language they need to hear? And how will they expand their understanding of the world in the way that it needs to be expanded? A read-aloud session can't take place without something to read. Books and stories have to be in the house— that's the first requirement.

Owning good books means children can read them over and over again, thereby gaining all the

benefits of the repetition of the stories. I know a child in Adelaide who read a favorite Dr. Seuss book until it was in tatters. His parents replaced it not once, but three times over seven years. Being able to own and read that particular book over and over for years made the child into a reader.

Going to a library is, of course, also essential, since most of us can't afford every book we like. Little Millie is the grandchild of a school librarian I know in Colorado, and needless to say, she loves libraries. In the car one Saturday morning when she was barely one and had just begun to talk, her father said, "We're going to the library, Millie."

"Book!" said Millie immediately, bouncing up and down. "Book! Book! Book!"

Millie's sublime ability to connect libraries to books and books to happiness at such an early age will give her a head start in life.

☆

We know that children like Millie who come from homes filled with books are more likely to succeed at school than children who don't. And the more books there are in a home, the more children can develop their own preferences and favorites. But where do we start? Which books will we choose? And where will we find them?

My book-obsessed husband is puzzled time and again by professional colleagues who ask: "So where can I buy Mem's new book?"

"Bookshops," he replies. "Any old bookshop. Or borrow them from libraries."

He wonders where they think books come from. Are bookshops and libraries so intimidating that people are scared to go into them? Surely they shouldn't be.

Having said that, I must admit I didn't know that plant nurseries existed until I became an avid gardener a few years ago. I had no idea plants could be bought anywhere except outside a hardware store until a gardening friend, astonished at my ignorance, took me under her wing. Perhaps finding books is similarly difficult for people who don't often look for them.

It doesn't have to be difficult. We could start with the magnificent book lists arranged in order of age appropriateness in *The Read-Aloud Handbook* by Jim Trelease or in *Valerie & Walter's Best Books for Children: A Lively, Opinionated Guide* by Valerie V. Lewis and Walter M. Mayes. Armed with this information, libraries and bookshops won't be so overwhelming. We can simply say, "Could you find me this book, please?" And if they don't have it, we can ask them to order it for us.

It's also a good idea to find a lively bookseller or passionate librarian who is eager to give advice and make suggestions. These people understand that every child has different interests at different times and that every child reads at his or her own level. And most important, they know books—new and old.

Making friends with a librarian or bookseller who gets to know our child is a great idea and saves a lot of time. We can then tap into their wisdom and depend upon them to put appropriate books aside for our children or order books for us if they're not available at that moment. When Chloë was in her teens, I relied heavily on a bookseller we knew for advice about books she might like. At the time I knew nothing about fiction for that age group.

Not everyone uses booksellers sensibly. Frank Hodge, owner of the renowned children's bookstore Hodge Podge Books in Albany, New York, often despairs about the inappropriate choices made by well-meaning adults on behalf of little kids. He wishes parents and others would listen more closely to his advice. After all, he's been in the book business for over forty years. In one of his recent newsletters, he wrote:

> The holiday season has ended and things will soon get back to normal. I do enjoy Christmas, but I get so frustrated with some of my customers. It seems everyone buying for that new and perfect grandchild thinks the kid is about to enter Harvard. The books they select for a two- and three-year-old would confound a graduate student. I try to show them books a kid might actually like, but their minds are set on a classic for little LeRoy or Hortense. It is a wonder some kids ever learn to read considering the materials they are faced with from their loving family members.

☆

There are many factors that determine whether a child will like a particular book. Children's choices relate to their own current passions, their stage of development, their state of mind, the time of day, how tired they are, the enthusiasm (or lack of it) from the adult reading the book, and so on.

So what is a good book, anyway? How do we decide?

When we're looking for books for babies and toddlers, we need to keep in mind that they love simple nonfiction books that illustrate and label familiar items on each page such as *hat, coat, shoes, umbrella.* And basic books about dinosaurs, volcanoes, heat and light, snakes, ancient Egypt, the weather, and so on are perfect for the young child who shows even an ounce of interest in such subjects. An interest sparked in early childhood can ignite a passion that lasts a lifetime.

In her late twenties, Chloë worked in Paris as a journalist for more than three years. It was not ideal, frankly, for parents of an only child to have that child living eleven thousand miles away, but whose fault was that? When she was three, we had read her a very simple nonfiction book called *France.* She loved it. Then we read her another book in the same series, *Sun.* She loved that, too, so we bought the same book in French, *Le soleil,* and read it to her. Then there was *Madeline,* set in Paris, and *The Beast of Monsieur Racine,* which also mentions Paris. An early interest in France turned into a lifelong passion. So if you want your toddlers to grow up and live next door—God forbid—don't read them books about the South American rain forest!

☆

Toddlers also adore very simple, clearly illustrated picture books such as the exciting *Rosie's Walk* by Pat Hutchins, which has a total of thirty-two words. And they delight in lift-the-flap books and in books with hilarious, detailed illustrations they can pore over tirelessly.

Nursery rhymes are of course a favorite with this age group, along with lively chants, easy songs, and finger games. Children will enjoy the nursery rhymes and songs—and learn them more quickly—if we're as physical as possible when we're reading, bouncing them on our knees, rocking them gently, or clapping hands, so our voices and their movements are synchronized.

It's useful to build on what children have gained

from all these rhymes and verses in their heads by next finding books with similar structures that swing from the stars on rhythm alone: books with strongly repeating patterns, or very clear rhymes, and language that's used curiously, in new or inventive ways. We'll be looking for outrageous words and phrases that children can appropriate into their own vocabularies, often hilariously. *Hop on Pop* by Dr. Seuss is a prime example of this sort of book. Its rhythm is addictive, partly because it's so bizarre.

I remember once driving along with my editor and her son, then aged three. He was tired and we had some distance to go, so Allyn and I were singing songs to keep him happy. But after a while Eamon spoke a line from *Hop on Pop,* firmly looking straight ahead.

"Good-by, Thing, you sing too long!"

No other sentence would have been quite as tactful at that moment. It was the perfect gentleman's choice, and Eamon had remembered it and been able to use it to get his point across because the rhymes and rhythms of *Hop on Pop* are dominant enough and wild enough to be unforgettable.

☆

Dr. Seuss books are never forgettable, but many picture books are. They're filled to the brim with cutesy-pie sentiment or are about nothing at all, when it comes down to it. We turn the last page and think: "Well, so what?"

A "so what" book is not a terrific book for kids. It will put them off books and reading altogether, which is the last thing we want to do. A terrific book matters to us as human beings. It's not terrific for adults or children if it leaves readers unmoved. It *is* terrific if we've had to shift around the furniture in our heads as we've listened, if it has affected us profoundly, one way or another—to laughter or tears, horror or delight, disgust or dismay, fascination or fright. If a book makes children laugh, cry, squeal, shiver, or wriggle and jiggle in some way, it takes up residence in their hearts and stays there.

When we look back and remember the books that linger in our own lives, it's more than likely that something fundamental in them touched us deeply. One such fundamental theme is trouble. "Trouble" means problems arising from the things that really matter to us, such as needing to be loved, not getting what we want, not belonging, striving for goals, being frightened, feeling sad, putting on an act for others, looking silly in public, wanting to be top dog, feeling jealous, wanting to be safe, hoping to be a star, and so on.

☆

It will do more for a child's literacy to own one much-loved, beautifully written, trouble-filled book than to own lots of tacky, unappealing books in which the child shows no interest. But any books that children own and love are good books *for them.*

One of my childhood favorites in the early fifties was a Little Golden Book called *Scuffy the Tugboat* by Gertrude Crampton. It certainly wasn't Great Literature, but it did have trouble in it, and it remains in print to this day. My heart still gives a little leap when I see the picture of Scuffy on the cover.

My dentist remembers a book called *A Pony for Tony* that his son loved to distraction. He had to read it to his son again and again, not skipping a page or a single word. The boy knew it by heart but still wanted it read aloud as often as anyone was willing to read it. The book apparently had very few redeeming qualities, but who cares? The child loved it and identified deeply with the character Tony, and that's what was important.

Identifying with the characters will draw children back to the same books often, for many unfathomable emotional reasons. Since we know that the repeated reading of a book is an important factor in literacy development, it's a huge bonus when children demand the same story again and again. And they'll make that demand if they like the characters, empathize with the characters, or see themselves in those characters.

A mother told me her daughter loved the character Koala Lou so much that after many readings the child insisted one day on waiting and waiting before they turned a particular page. Koala Lou had just climbed the gum tree with apparent triumph in the Bush Olympics. On the next page, the child knew, lay disaster. Koala Lou would not have won after all.

"Wait, wait!" said the child. "Don't turn the page yet."

"Why not?" asked the mother.

"If we wait, this time she might WIN!"

I remember a similar experience when my niece, Tami, was "reading" *The Giant Devil Dingo* by Dick Roughsey, a book she knew well. She was three at the time. The book was open to the dramatic picture of the giant devil dingo coming around the side of a mountain. Tami sat there, waiting, not turning the page.

"What's the matter?" I asked.

"I'm just waiting for the dingo to go away. He's scary."

Such reactions are a joy. They show that the characters in these books took on a life of their own, entered two children's hearts, and stayed.

☆

When we're deciding whether to borrow or buy a book, the best way to sift its contents and discover the essence of its goodness, as well as its impurities, is— surprise!—to read it aloud. We can learn to discriminate pretty quickly between a good book and a bad one if we take the time to sit down with a large pile and read them aloud. The dull ones will be obvious right away. And if we're reading in a jerky fashion, or tripping up over sentences, or having to reread to clarify a rhythm, then the book isn't good enough, either—the words have not been perfectly chosen nor perfectly placed. We need to look for books that tell a good story *and* play with language.

It won't be difficult deciding which books to take home. The really good ones won't let us leave without them.

For parents still wondering, "Which books?" it is a good idea to set up a reading group with other parents that meets occasionally and shares surefire children's books by reading them aloud to each other. Adults are quickly hooked by children's books when they're exposed to the best of them.

☆

So far, I haven't mentioned fairy tales. But they're extremely important and mustn't be forgotten. Einstein himself told the story of a woman who'd asked what she could do to make her son more intelligent.

"Read him fairy stories," he said.

The woman, thinking he was being lighthearted, laughed and said: "And when I've read him fairy stories, then what should I do?"

Einstein replied: "Read him more fairy stories."

Fairy stories require the mind to be attentive to detail, to be highly active in problem solving, to roll through tunnels of prediction and meaning making, and to tumble down hills of emotion and run back up again.

Fairy tales often appear collected in fat books with few illustrations. This lack of pictures makes fairy

tales particularly special because children's imaginations have to work a little harder when they hear the stories. As children listen spellbound to the words, they have to use their brains actively to create their own pictures, thereby developing the all-important imagination that Einstein was so keen to promote.

(I often tell stories rather than read them. There is no book. There are no illustrations. And some of the children who listen, whose imaginations have been mashed by endless television watching, have a hard time creating the scenes and characters and events in their heads. Once in a hushed, desperate moment halfway through a story that I was telling, a child sitting at the back called out: "I can't see! I can't see!" without realizing there was no book to see. Such a child, through no fault of her own, has a rusty brain at an early age and may never reach her intellectual potential.)

Fairy tales—like the best picture books and novels—provide children with rules for living. They uplift us all with their grand examples of love and sorrow, courage and fortitude, being brave against the odds, living by one's wits, and caring for the downtrodden. They're the best sermons in literature, thundering into children's memories and remaining there as signposts to a well-lived life. (Experts tell us that many young criminals who have never been exposed to the cause-and-effect elements that abound in stories—particularly fairy tales—literally cannot imagine the consequences of their crimes. To correct this, some rehabilitation programs actually include reading stories aloud to young offenders.)

In *The Uses of Enchantment,* Bruno Bettelheim tells us that fairy tales are so important to human social development that we ought to be reading them as often as possible, and the ones we choose should be

the original blood-and-guts versions, not the simper-
ing, sanitized, sugar-sweet versions.

While children are listening to these often horrify-
ing fairy tales, they will become silent, fascinated, upset, appalled, aghast, and may even cry. But if they feel
deliciously safe with us while the story is being read—
and indeed this is essential—the more often they will
want to relive the drama. In frightening stories, it's
someone else's drama, which is why frightening stories

horacek

are so appealing. And in the end, the child is rescued by a life buoy of happiness when the good live happily ever after, and the bad come to a sticky end.

Experiencing this heightened level of emotion through literature is seen by some squeamish parents and educators as a Bad Thing. But child psychologists disagree. The whole point of books is to allow us to experience troubled realities that are different from our own, to feel the appropriate emotions, to empathize, to make judgments, and to have our interest held. If we sanitize everything children read, how much more shocking and confusing will the real world be when they finally have to face it?

☆

CHAPTER FOURTEEN

Television:
The Good, the Bad,
and the Ugly

Reading is not inherently "good." Television is not inherently "bad." What matters for children—and adults—is the pleasure, the experiences, the relaxation, the excitement, the workings of the brain, the growth in general knowledge, and the satisfaction they get from each.

Most of us lash ourselves with guilt about letting our children watch too much television. Without doubt, television sets should be banned from children's bedrooms if we want them to love books and become lifelong readers, but getting rid of television altogether would be absurd, unnecessary, and undesirable. Neither television nor the Internet will go away. They're here to stay, and their attractions are many.

Children gain enormously from good television.

Hundreds of unknown worlds and different experiences are revealed to them, providing valuable insights that expand their minds and are a great help when they begin to learn to read. Clearly the enriching value of television shouldn't be dismissed.

(However, if children watch television in the mornings before they leave for school, they should watch only the gentlest and slowest kinds of programs that treat children as clever, inquisitive beings, rather than as idiot consumers. Morning television of the cheap, fast, screamy-screamy kind seriously harms kids' ability to concentrate later in the day. It dulls their brains and sets up dangerous expectations of school that won't be met: fast patter, changing lights and colors, yelling voice-overs, quick changes of topic—things that simply don't occur in most normal classrooms.)

☆

Rather than indulging in nail-biting anxiety about TV, we might do better to focus on what we can do about *reading* in order to make it as attractive as television.

I have a young acquaintance who was so addicted to television that she never read a book, even though she could read. Her mother contacted me in some anxiety because she was dropping behind her class-mates at school. The first thing I discovered was that she wasn't allowed to read in bed!

She certainly had a lamp nearby in case she woke up in the night and was frightened. And she had books on her shelves—her mother had seen to that. But she had no encouragement to read, nor the time to read, nor a quiet place to read in. The television in her house was always on, and in winter there was no warm place to read because the warmest room had the television in it. There was no comfortable sofa she could curl up and read on because the only sofa was in the warm, well-lit, comfortable, noisy room that had the television in it. And there was no cool place in the summer, because once again the coolest room in the house—the one with the comfortable sofa in it—also had the television.

The mother's anxiety about her daughter's read-ing level was very real. She thought she had a big problem on her hands, but when the child was given these essentials: encouragement, time, books, maga-zines, light, silence, warmth in winter and coolness in summer, and the comfort of being allowed to read in bed every night, the problem was solved.

☆

From a child's point of view, one of the best things about television is that it isn't competitive. There's no such thing as a good television watcher or a bad television watcher. No one has any idea about our capabilities as television watchers—no one is better than we are, or worse. And no parent stands at the school gate and says proudly to another parent: "Brett's been put in the top television-watching group. We're so thrilled!"

But in school every child knows who the best readers are—and the worst. Reading schemes are designed in such a way that the entire class knows that the slowest kids are still on low-level readers in third grade. These children's shame pervades the classroom and alters their lives by making them a public failure. Is it surprising that they prefer watching television?

I'm reminded of a little girl in Adelaide who said she hated reading. When asked why, she replied: "My legs get tired." She had obviously been asked too often to read aloud in a physically and emotionally cold environment, standing in some discomfort at the teacher's desk, waiting in dread to be corrected at every second word. Who ever *stands up* watching television for any length of time?

This poor child has learned to associate books with fear, shame, and boredom. When did television ever fill children with fear, shame, and boredom? No wonder she prefers television!

Of course she will also prefer watching television to reading if she is being forced to work her way through school readers that have puzzling language, uninspired plots, and banal illustrations. There is no comparison between the entertainment value of one and the tedium of the other.

☆

When Chloë was in first grade, the school expected her to grind her way through a hierarchy of readers. She would insist on reading aloud to us the required number of pages every night, even though it was ridiculous and unnecessary—she was already reading picture books fluently.

The worst aspect of this exercise was the manner of her reading aloud. Instead of reading with lively expression as she did normally, she did it in the stilted manner of a child who's beginning to decode the words on the page for the first time:

"Tim • and • Pat • and • Ro • ver • went • to • the • park • to • play."

"Why are you reading like that, for heaven's sake?" I asked.

"Because that's the way you *have* to read at school, silly!"

I laughed so much she burst into tears. Malcolm had to listen to her nightly school reading after that. I couldn't stand the stress. Nor could I bear to think that this activity might put her off books altogether. No school ever says: "You *have* to watch this amount of television tonight." We watch it because we want to. And television *never* produces this sort of strain, which is another reason kids love it.

They will love books too, of course, if we continue to read them brilliant stuff from excellent authors whose writing appeals, touches lives, and lingers.

CHAPTER FIFTEEN

☆

Troubleshooting

Our darling toddlers can't stay at home being read aloud to forever. They have to move on and up into school. This can be a thrilling experience or one that dashes their hopes, depending on the school and the methods it uses to teach reading and writing.

When a child experiences difficulty in learning to read at school, our first impulse is to blame the child. That's most unfair. The book he or she is trying to read may be hideously illustrated, or badly written, or too difficult, or a total yawn: a school reader for example. When such a book is put in front of a failing child, everything becomes tense: her body, her brain, her teacher, the situation, the very air itself. There's no fun left anymore. No time for *that*. There's not much learning left, either—the child is too petrified and turned off.

Another problem might lie in the relationship between the adult and the book being read—the adult may loathe the book because it's so boring and pointless. This loathing may translate into impatience and irritation with the child who is struggling.

Yet another problem might be a relationship breakdown between the child and the adult. To put it tactfully, the adult—the teacher perhaps—and the child may not get along. To put it truthfully, they may detest each other. In such a situation, successful, happy reading is not going to take place.

☆

There is a group of puzzling children who don't *want* to learn to read, even though they have for years loved listening to books being read. Many, though not all, of these children are the second or a later child in the family. They have, naturally, vastly appreciated the individual parental attention and warmth during their bedtime read-aloud sessions. Subconsciously, they may believe that if they learn to read, this special attention will disappear. They don't realize that their parents will continue to read aloud to them for as many years as possible—whether they can read or not—because the benefits are so extraordinary. We need to make sure they know we won't stop reading aloud to them once they learn to read by themselves.

These children may take their time learning to read, but they do learn eventually. The reading aloud they love will always be a major benefit to their literacy development, no matter how long it takes for their literacy to flower.

☆

Not all reading problems are relationship based. Some children do make a lot of mistakes when they're reading, and that's a problem. Should we correct them? On the whole, kids who have been read to regularly will not read nonsense because they know that writing makes sense. They've heard words making sense for far too long *not* to know that. They might, in their haste, say *home* when the text says *house*, but that's all right, and should be left alone, because the meaning is more or less correct.

But if they make really silly errors or read total

nonsense such as "moon the yellow grow isn't then dump," the story is probably too difficult. They should be eased off that particular book with tact, and they'll certainly need to hear it *read aloud* more often.

☆

Sometimes when children can't work out a word that they're reading, they will look up for assistance. Without getting twitchy about it, we need to attempt to focus their eyes back to the print, to train them into knowing that's where the secrets of reading lie, not in the air around us, or on our faces.

They must learn that looking at the words should provide the help they need. If they look at the word and still can't say it, we shouldn't hang about waiting; we should tell them what it is, while at the same time making very sure they're *looking at the word* when we say it.

The more we read a particular book aloud to them before they read it themselves, the less they will look up for help. They'll instead be able to use the information they've stored in their memories, as well as the print on the page, their knowledge of language, and their general knowledge to help them figure out any difficult words.

☆

When a child is reading aloud to us with great aplomb and mostly correctly, it's very tempting to comment only when the child slips up and makes a mistake, as if mistakes are all we're listening for. This is very discouraging for young readers, especially ones who are struggling. We need to watch our behavior in these situations and be encouraging instead, with comments like "good," "terrific!," "excellent," and "well done!" during the reading.

(Having said that, though, let's not skirt around the issue of overpraising. Too much praise of faint achievement isn't good for children. We need to be truthful or we'll give them a false idea of their capabilities, which may cause them to feel resentful and disappointed in later life. They'll feel they've been cheated somehow if they're constantly told they're a big success and then discover in the end that it wasn't always true. Nevertheless, when there's reading or writing happening in our homes, being positive and having fun have to be uppermost in our tired minds.)

☆

If a child reads a *favorite* book incorrectly over and over again, we might be tempted to force the issue by getting terribly severe and making the child concentrate on reading the right words at the right time. After all, they can't go on forever reading the wrong words! But let's go gently at this point. If we start getting anxious and nasty over books and reading, all the love, the playing, and the happiness will be lost from our reading experiences, which would be disastrous. The child may simply need to hear the story read aloud a lot more. Or we might like to play a focus-on-the-letters-and-words game.

For example, the parent could read the book and then say to the child: "You choose a word in the book, any word, and I'll tell you what letter it starts with. Then I'll choose a word, and you can tell me what letter it starts with. But there's a trick. We can't use the same letter twice, so you'd better keep a list of the letters we use. If anyone uses the same letter twice, they lose." This game has the child writing the individual letters of the alphabet for a real reason.

As parent and child play the game, the parent reads aloud every word that is chosen, whether it's his turn or the child's. He makes sure the child can identify the words. He praises the child for every attempt. He makes sure he loses the game by being the one to choose the same letter twice. He helps the child write the list of used letters. And he gets really excited, because it is exciting, and he's getting *correctly* into the child's head the words he or she has been reading incorrectly.

Any reluctance on the part of the child to play the game should not be ignored. If the child won't play, then the parent shouldn't insist. He should just continue to read aloud.

☆

As I said at the beginning of this chapter, it's unjust to lay the blame on children when they fail to become readers. It's too easy to call these hapless kids "reading disabled" or "learning disabled." It might be more appropriate to call them "book-choice disabled" or "relationship disabled" or, in some circumstances, even "teacher disabled." Through no fault of their own, these so-called "disabled" children take years longer than normal to learn to read. And some never learn. Their reading problems at school are often disguised by their panic-stricken parents under the socially acceptable label of "dyslexia." I'm not denying that some children and adults really do have dyslexia. But it's an overused excuse.

Anxiety should set in only when a child of eight can't read. By eight going on nine, professional help might be needed, but whatever happens, *pressure should be taken off the child entirely.* Pressure and a sense of failure are no help at all to learners. The aim should be to make reading seem as fabulous as it is for most of us: fun, hilarious, thrilling, useful, interesting, amazing, essential, and desirable.

☆

Whatever happens in the world of school, continuing to read aloud to our children at home should solve most reading problems and will always be a lifeline to their happiness, their literacy, and their future.

CHAPTER SIXTEEN

☆

Phokissing on Fonix

My name is an example of easy phonics: *M-e-m F-o-x.*
But *bough, cough, through, tough* and *though* are a phonics nightmare—each "identical" ending has a different pronunciation.

But what is phonics, exactly? In order to avoid
misunderstandings as our children move into school
we need to be able to define the terms associated
with various methods in the teaching of reading (although research tells us it's not the method so much
as the teacher that makes the difference).

Phonics is the ability to translate the print on the
page into sound: for example, seeing the word *cat* on
the page and saying *cat;* or being able to break it up
into sounds and saying: *kuh-a-tuh.*

Some languages are more phonically simple than others: Finnish and Bahasa Indonesian for instance, are easier to "read" than French or English. Only 50 percent of English words are phonically simple; that is, only 50 percent can be sounded out easily. For instance, neither of these ordinary words: *you* or *beautiful* can be sounded out phonically. And why isn't *beautiful* spelled *b-you-tiful*? After all it would make sense. The problem is that English spelling doesn't make sense.

Phonics is often confused with "phonetics" which is a totally different branch of language study. It has nothing to do with reading. Phonetics is a method of interpreting the various sounds of language, such as the broad Australian *loyt* for *light*, into weird written symbols.

☆

Occasionally we may hear the term "whole word" in relation to the teaching of reading. When this method was in vogue more than forty years ago it was called the "look and say" method: children looked at individual, disconnected words on charts or cards and chanted them out after the teacher.

In this minefield of different terms "whole word" is often confused with the more recent "whole language" method.

"Whole language" teaching was so named in the early eighties for several reasons. The teaching of reading began by engaging children in "whole" stories read aloud by the teacher, real stories that children heard again and again and learned to love. These stories captured children's hearts and minds and made them eager to learn to read. From whole stories teachers then focused on sentences within those stories, then words within those sentences, and finally on the parts of those words: the phonics. But always the phonics, the words, and the sentences made sense since they related back to something that had meaning to the children: a story they loved.

Whole language was also "whole" in that the teaching of reading happened at the same time children learned to read and write. The whole of literacy was taught simultaneously: reading, writing, speaking, listening, and viewing.

Over the years the term "whole language" became so misunderstood by both teachers and the public that it's now more often called "balanced literacy." This method, currently in use in the most successful classrooms in Canada, Australia, and New Zealand has meant that these three countries now have the highest literacy rates in the world after Finland.

☆

My neighborhood wonder-girl Josephine, who can read anything at the age of three, did not learn to read with phonics.

She came around to see me one day, with her mother, to say how much she loved my book *Koala Lou*. She read me the whole book, self-correcting when she needed to. A couple of days later she read to me perfectly, sight unseen, from an adult book on dream interpretation.

Josephine's dad is an accountant and her mother is in human resources. Neither has been an educator. They told me they didn't know how it had happened. When I asked if they had read aloud to her, they both said: "Of course. All the time! Ever since she was born."

Josephine was read the same stories repeatedly, many hundreds of times. Her mother told me that Josie taught herself to read using whole words. She did not use phonics to learn new words and is very confused if this method is thrust upon her. When someone tells her that *hot* is made up of the sounds *huh-o-tuh*, Josie quite rightly hears *her otter* instead of *hot*. When she doesn't know a word she asks what it is, and remembers it the next time she sees it. From the words she already knows she applies logic to extrapolate what other words will be in the sentence she's reading.

☆

This is exactly how Chloë learnt to read, two weeks after she started school, aged four and a half. She'd heard the same favorite books read time and time again, and watched the print, and joined in. And then, like the prima donna she was, she demanded that she be allowed to read them herself, preferably on audiotape so she could listen to herself later! When she didn't know a word I told her what it was immediately so she could keep the story going, storming ahead with blind courage.

"You will *tell* me the difficult words, won't you, Mummy?" she'd say as she launched, pell-mell and fearlessly, into reading a story she loved. I remember two words in particular at which she hesitated: *cozy* and *investigation*. I told her what they were. A few pages later, when the same words reappeared, she read them without any hesitation whatsoever.

☆

Looking back on all the print and language and books and love that surrounded Chloë, it would have been remarkable if she *hadn't* learned to read at four. The fact that she did no longer surprises me.

Three-year-old Josie doesn't surprise me either. She's developed an understanding of what the text should say when she encounters a new word. She's listened to literary and spoken language so regularly, from being read aloud to so much, that she has an innate sense of what's appropriate. She takes into account what she's reading and applies commonsense as to what a word will probably be, and then looks at the print to confirm her hunch. That's what all competent readers do: you're doing it right now as you read this sentence.

When children learn to read before school without any lessons, they do so because they've been looking at the same print as they've listened to the same language in the same stories, which have been read again and again. Not only does the print become familiar, language becomes familiar. Learning to read is more about learning language than it is about making sounds from the letters on a page.

☆

Let's assume that learning to read is like driving a car. Most adults can drive, but only a tiny proportion of us would be able to take a car to pieces, lay all the pieces out along a road, and then put the car together again so that it worked well enough to drive us to our required destination. Teaching children to read through a phonics-only program is asking them to take reading to pieces and then put it together again. Not only is that difficult and horribly confusing, it's unnecessary.

☆

If Josie didn't learn to read through phonics, is phonics essential to reading? The answer is: sometimes. But a capability in phonics doesn't necessarily mean a child (or an adult) can read, or is reading. Getting the sound right proves nothing: *the meaning is on the page, not in the sound.*

It is possible to "read" with all the right phonics in place but not make any sense out of what we're reading aloud. I can correctly read aloud an Indonesian sentence from my picture book *Shoes from Grandpa* without having a clue as to its meaning, and so can you:

"Terima kasih banyak, kakek!" kata Jessie. ("Thanks a lot, Grandpa," said Jessie.) If I understood Bahasa I could *really* read the sentence because I'd be able to make the right sounds and make sense out of it as well.

☆

Now the big problem is that many politicians, media commentators, writers of expensive reading schemes and quick-fix cures for reading, and even a few teachers and university academics think that sounding out *is* reading. But if that's the case, I ask again, why do most of us read successfully, in silence? We manage it because *the meaning is on the page, not in the sound.*

☆

English is a wickedly confusing language since so many words look exactly the same, like c-l-o-s-e in: *Close the door,* and: *Wow, that was close!* We need to grab the meaning and the pronunciation by knowing the context, or seeing the word in a sentence, since *close* on its own isn't enough. Dozens of similar examples litter the English language, thereby confusing not only foreigners learning English, but also young children learning to read.

☆

Phonics doesn't take account of different English accents either. In Australia I'm an *ortha* (author), but in America I'm an *arthurrrr.* Whose phonics is correct? Does *au* sound like *or*? Or does it sound like *ar*? The sound *au* is also problematic in the words *author* and *laugh.* Which is correct? How can we know until we see the *au* in a word?

Once when I was in the southern United States I made a dreadful mistake at a book signing. I signed a book, as instructed, to "Terror." I must admit I thought it an odd name. The owner of the book was devastated.

"No, no," she said. "I meant *Terror.*"

"Well, that's what I've written!" I said.

"No, like this." And on a piece of paper she wrote "Tara," which I pronounce as *Tah-ra.* **The meaning was on the page, not in the sound.**

I had to buy her a new book.

More recently I signed a book for another Tara, this time in Minnesota, in the Midwest of the United States. I was surprised to find that in Minnesota *Tara* was pronounced just as I pronounce it: *Tah-ra.* Once again I realized that phonics is not a single stable entity: It moves. It changes from state to state and from English-speaking country to English-speaking country. Because it varies for speakers of different dialects or accents, it's crazy to assume that one phonics program is appropriate for every speaker or reader wherever English is spoken.

☆

If phonics is so fundamental to our ability to make meaning from text, as so many claim, why can we read and understand the next two paragraphs so easily and quickly?

Aoccdrnig to rscheearch at an Elingsh
uinervtisy, it deosn't mttaer in waht oredr the
ltteers in a wrod are, the olny iprmoetnt tihng
is that the frist and lsat ltteers are in the rghit
pclae: the rset can be a toatl mses but you can
still raed it wouthit a porbelm. This is bcuseae
we don't raed ervey lteter but the word as a
wlohe.

So, hey, waht does this say abuot the
improtnace of phnoics in raeidng? Prorbalby
that phonics ins't very imoptrnat at all.
How apcoltapyic is *that*, in the cuerrnt licetary
wars!

☆

As if that weren't proof enough that phonics is useful
but not essential, here's more: How can it be possible
that the billions of people in China, Japan, Korea,
and Taiwan learn to read when there is no phonics
possible in their written language, which is displayed,
instead, in picture symbols called "pictographs"?

I posed this question to Jürgen Kracht, a close
friend who teaches Chinese at a private school in
Adelaide. He told me that children in China have to

be told what a word is, and then learn to recognize it and memorize it.

☆

It transpires that children like Josephine who learn to read before school without any lessons *never sound out words phonically as they learn to read.* In other words, advanced readers don't use phonics, even at the age of three! They use phonics only *after* they have learned to read, when they meet difficult, multisyllabic words that they can't make sense of by the usual logical means: through print, or grammar, or context, or a prior understanding of what they have just read, or through general knowledge.

We do need phonics, of course, as soon as we learn to write, aged about four or five, when we struggle to make meaning by matching the sounds of language to the letters we scrawl across a page. It's during this complex struggle that we learn our phonics and then our spelling.

In effective classrooms children are learning to write at the same time as they are being read to from "big books" (so they can all see the print as they hear the story), that is, at the same time as they are learning to read on their own. If learning to read and learning to write go hand in hand, children's literacy advances enormously.

Here are a few sentences from letters to me written by children in their first year at school. We can "hear" the southern United States accent in the first example and the Canadian accent in the second—and we can observe their gorgeously clever struggle with phonics:

- *I hop you are dowen fan.* (I hope you are doing fine.)
- *Dare mem fox I love your books and you are good raider and you are a nis girl.* (Dear Mem Fox I love your books and you are a good writer and you are a nice girl.)
- *I lict yur books.* (I liked your books.)

☆

As adults we use phonics whenever we encounter an unfamiliar, multisyllabic word, or we spell a word incorrectly. For instance, I can never spell Wollongong. The first time I type it I get too many *o*'s or *l*'s in it: *Wollongongong.* I have to break it up phonically, saying it aloud, to get it right.

☆

"Synthetic" phonics is being able to read meaningless words like *vit, rog,* or *jat.* But how does it help a child or an adult reader to be able to read purely phonic words such as these if there's no meaning in them? Synthetic phonics takes the meaning out of reading, which is another way of saying that it takes the *reading* out of reading. All that's left is the empty ability to make sounds from symbols on a page.

☆

When we force children, usually struggling readers, to sound out words they don't know instead of simply telling them the word, these little kids read so slowly that they make almost no sense out of the print they are "decoding." Children who are reluctant, remedial readers may be able, tortuously, to complete a little book phonically, but there's no joy in it, no excitement or passion or emotion of any kind, and ultimately no reward.

"If that's reading," they seem to be saying to themselves, "then who needs it?" Ironically, teachers tend to teach phonics heavily to the very children who need phonics least: the ones who can't yet read, the ones who have never "had a ride in the literacy car" but are still trying to put the pieces of the car together, in mind-numbing boredom.

☆

If children are exposed to books, print, pictures, page-turning and gorgeous stories that lighten up their lives, and fabulous crazy-wild-happy teachers who switch them on to loving books, they will long to learn to read. A phonics-only approach can never, in its wildest dreams, achieve this goal.

Do we want children who have lacked books and happy read-alouds in their first five years to arrive at school and be resurrected into lifelong literacy, or do we want these keen little kids to be crucified on the cross of meaningless phonics?

We all know the answer to that question.

CHAPTER SEVENTEEN

☆

Boys and Reading

When we hear the words: "It's a boy!" we should immediately thrill to the expectation that our son(s) will adore being read to and will fall in love with books just as quickly as the other half of the human race.

The secret to boys and reading is to get 'em young. We need to mesmerize baby boys in the first months of their lives with the rhyme, rhythm, and repetition that's so common in books for the very young. If boys (and girls, of course) are read to often in their bassinets with joy and noisy love, and also with soothing sweetness, we hook them into associating books with happiness before they can crawl away from us to explore the rest of the world.

☆

A colleague of mine, Lorraine, had two sons, three years apart. When she was breastfeeding her baby, she would read to Nathan, the older child, so he wouldn't feel left out. Nathan would change sides as the baby changed breasts. As a result, baby Rowan was listening to the stories of Eric Carle, Maurice Sendak, and John Burningham on a daily basis from the age of five days. He loved books as a child and learned to read before he was five. When Lorraine bought him his own bedlamp so he could read in bed, he drew her a card that said it was his best present ever. At twenty-eight, Rowan still loves reading because he literally couldn't escape from books as a baby.

☆

As boys grow older there will be times when they don't seem to be interested in reading: for example, between twelve and eighteen months their concentration will be all over the place. That's normal. And they won't want to be read to if there's a fascinating electric plug to poke at, or another child to play with. There is one time of day, however, when reading aloud will not fail: bedtime, when the run-around boy is so exhausted he can't move. His eyes are closing, his

breathing is slowing—gotcha! Our comforting presence and soothing voice will wash over him as his favorite stories lull him to blissful sleep.

I know a boy called Matthew who so loved being
read to that when he moved out of his cot his parents
bought him an extra-large single bed so they could lie
down beside him to read aloud. It was a rest time for
them, as well as bedtime for their son. Not surprisingly, he learned to read at the age of four without
any lessons. Matthew so loved this nighttime routine
that he wanted the reading time to continue. He is
nine now, and one of his parents (they take it in
turns) still lies down with him at night and they both
read a book, a different book, side by side.

☆

We do need to ensure that it's not always a quiet reading aloud, with the passive child taking no part. It's
important to read the same stories again and again,
letting the child join in with gusto. When the appropriate moments arise we'll talk about the individual
words: "Yes, that says BEAR! You can say BEAR! if you
like." And we'll bang the book where the word BEAR!
appears. "And yes, that says KANGAROO, clever boy!"

And if it's a Matthew we're reading to, we'll eventually point out the letter M for his name, and then perhaps other letters of interest, always playing, always
laughing and having a great time.

A dad told me once that he read to his daughter
totally differently after he'd heard me read aloud:
"Man, we have FUN! I used to read in such a dull way
that I kind of hated reading aloud and my daughter
didn't like it much either."

☆

Fun must have happened in Sean's house. His mother
Angie wrote to say:

> *Your books hold a special place in our lives,*
> *wonderful memories of baby and early childhood.*
> *Our son was able to read Grade Two readers at three*
> *years. I read to him every day from five months on*
> *and now he reads to his baby sister, and has done so*
> *from the time she was two days old. I followed your*
> *advice and think* Reading Magic *is one of the most*
> *valuable books ever!*

I contacted Angie and she repeated the same old
read-aloud story, a story that never ceases to excite

me, no matter how often I hear it. She told me she was reading to Sean at five months old and that *Time for Bed* was the first of my books she bought. She thinks she read *Reading Magic* when Sean was almost two years old. She said she was an instant convert. (I believe she had converted herself before she'd read my book.) She couldn't get over the fact that it could be so simple and told all her friends about it.

Sean's reading developed very quickly. At three years and seven months he had a reading age of seven years and seven months, and the verbal understanding of a child of fourteen and a half. Angie claimed it was merely from doing the things I'd recommended.

Sean appeared in a program on national television in a segment called "Genius Kid," and no wonder. He has an IQ of 147 and he's already been accepted into Mensa, aged five. Angie said: "He just seems to be good at everything but he's a perfectly normal loving child." Sean now reads up to ten books a day.

☆

At this point it's important to recall that learning to read is a joy, not a race. Most children don't learn to read at home. They learn soon after they start school, when everything they already know clicks into place with the help of an excellent teacher. But many girls *and* boys are learning to read before they start school and they're learning quickly, happily and easily, like Sean, Matthew, and Rowan. The big thing to remember is to read aloud with happiness in mind, not education. We'll get it all wrong if we think only about education. Learning to read comes from the happiness of reading.

☆

This brings us to bonding. Recent research from Oxford University tells us that love is essential to brain development; that when mothers in particular resent their children, or are highly upset and stressed by other troubles in their lives, a baby's brain is adversely affected in ways that change the child's life forever. It's dismaying to realize that if certain connections aren't made in a baby's brain in the first year of life, they are unlikely to be made later, and the child will be affected socially, physically, and educationally. The first year of life is the great window of opportunity and it shouldn't be missed.

So if it's important for mothers and fathers to bond with their sons (and their daughters), reading aloud is a helpful strategy. It's almost impossible not to relate to a child when we're reading aloud to him (or her). Or singing to him. Or chatting to him. Or playing clapping rhymes and other games. Or hugging him and murmuring in his ear, or kissing the back of his perfect little neck.

Read-aloud sessions are times when parents and children fall in love with each other. Parents who read aloud regularly to their children get to know their kids well and dote on them more because the things little kids say and do during a read-aloud are so funny and adorable. People who tell me they haven't got time to read aloud every day for ten minutes make me choke. We have to make time. After all, it's fun! It's hilarious! It's gorgeous!

Bonding through books also helps the brain to develop. It's hard to read to a baby without holding it, and touch is known to be the most important of the five senses for setting down the neural pathways to learning, especially in the first four months of life.

☆

Reading aloud to our sons (and daughters) also helps them to learn the best kinds of universal values, which will help them grow into being pleasant children now, and good citizens later. It advances their speech, enlarges their brain, makes them happy, and helps them to be successful at school and in life. It also gives them sky-high self-esteem. They realize that we love them dearly.

☆

But what if it's mothers who are doing all the reading? We're all aware of the current anxiety about boys and their education; about the preponderance of female teachers in primary schools; about boys not having enough male role models. If mothers are the only ones reading aloud, reading will be seen as an activity valued only by females. This attitude will be reinforced in schools as a result of the imbalance of female-to-male teachers. If reading is viewed as a highly gendered activity our society is in trouble. (Mind you, look at all the boys avidly reading the Harry Potter series!)

If we want boys to fulfill their educational potential, we have to begin to focus on fathers reading aloud to their sons. All the talk about what happens at school with male role models for boys is five years too late in a boy's life. It's fathers who need to be there from the start, reading aloud and showing love to their kids from the first hours of their lives; and thereafter as often as they can (or at least at bedtimes) for the next five years. This is possible whether parents are together or divorced, even if a parent only sees the children every other week.

☆

There's a belief that fathers like to bond with their sons by kicking a ball around the backyard. Apart from the fact that this doesn't address the issue of fathers bonding with their daughters, there are a couple of other points to be made about this assumption.

First, not all fathers and sons kick a ball around the backyard. Some fathers don't engage in sports. Some sons don't either.

Second, kicking a ball around the backyard can be done with little or no talk. It's a physical activity, great for the body and good fun, but it's not great for developing a line of communication between a parent and a child. Kicking a ball around can be a way of *not* talking about things that matter, such as hopes and fears, troubles and triumphs. Kicking a ball around doesn't provide a window into a child's mind, or into his heart. Reading aloud to him does.

☆

Here's a sad story about a father called Frank, not his real name, who's a waiter at a restaurant we frequent. Many months after we'd met him he revealed he had three young children. Young children? And I didn't know! There were parents to whom I hadn't given my "Mem Fox Starter Pack" of *Reading Magic, Time for Bed,* and *Where Is The Green Sheep?* Good grief!

"Frank!" I said in mock horror. "How come I haven't signed any books for your kids? This is appalling!" He laughed and said it was OK, they did have four hundred books, and they were being read aloud to.

"Which Mem Fox books have they got?" I asked. "I'll give you ones they don't already have."

"I'll ask my wife," he said. "She's the one who reads aloud to them."

So Frank doesn't read aloud to his kids. But why should mothers have the exclusive right to bond with their children? Children are desperate to know they're loved and valued by their mothers *and* their fathers. Frank doesn't realize how much his kids would love it if he spent more time with them reading aloud, chatting, laughing, bonding and getting wildly excited about their happy progress.

☆

I generally refuse to sign *Reading Magic* to a mother only, unless she's a single mother. If there's a father anywhere on the horizon I insist on signing the book to him too. He is not equally important, he is *more* important in this read-aloud world, because he needs to bond with his sons and daughters, whom he may not see or interact with as often as his wife or partner does.

☆

A colleague of mine, Dr. McDonald, once suggested to an anxious mother of an eight-year-old, nonreading boy that the *father* read aloud to their son each night, instead of *her.* The mother said that although her husband played sports with their son he didn't have time to read aloud to him as he was always home late from work.

Dr. McDonald insisted. She said that having the father read to the son, even once or twice a week, or at weekends, anything that demonstrated a male enjoying reading, would probably be the most significant factor in getting the boy to read. About a month later the mother told Dr. McDonald that her suggestion had changed the family dynamics. The father had come to love sharing this time with his son and now came home earlier to read to him every night. And one evening, out of the blue, their son had read them the football headlines from the paper.

I had a similar experience myself. During a signing in 2005, when the queues went on forever and I was trying not to hold up the line by chatting too long, a woman said: "*Reading Magic* changed my life." My heart rose and sank at the same time. Did I have time to hear the story? I made the time to listen.

She told me her son had been a nonreader at nine. His inability to read had been causing him great grief, and his parents huge embarrassment. Her son had been on the verge of being placed in a special class at school. Then she read *Reading Magic* and thought its suggestions might be the answer to her prayers; but she thought the ideas would work better if the father read to the child because the boy idolized his dad.

It took her four months to persuade her husband to read *Reading Magic,* but when he finally did he took its passions to heart. The son's reading took off to such an extent that by ten and a half he couldn't keep his nose out of a book.

"But the best thing of all," said the mother, and she started to cry, "the best thing, the most unexpected thing, was that my husband and my son now have a really loving relationship. They'd never had that before." At that point I cried too!

Which makes this message from Sue on my Web site all the more poignant:

Reading Magic *has brought about a revelation in my house—my children and I sit down each day (at least twice a day) and we enjoy reading a couple of books together in each session. I'd forgotten how much fun reading aloud can be, and no longer see this as an onerous task, but as an enjoyable time of day that we all look forward to. And lo and behold, my son (aged three) read* Rascal the Dragon *by Paul Jennings to me after our second session—he*

loves it, and even though he's not reading verbatim,
he is enjoying retelling the story in his own words.

Thank you, thank you, thank you for making
reading such an enjoyable experience for us—now
I just need to work on Daddy to join in the fun!

☆

In 2004 Mark Latham succeeded in raising awareness across Australia about the sensational benefits of reading aloud but did admit to feeling like an idiot at first, reading aloud to his four-month-old son, Oliver:

I say to parents who might think that there is time
to wait, and that this is the sort of thing that can be
delayed to age three or four: it is true that in those
early months you will feel a bit dorky holding the
child and trying to get them used to the book, and
there will be times when the child will grab the book
and try and eat it, chew it or tear it, but persevere,
because it is worthwhile. It is absolutely worthwhile.

☆

I was at a function recently, sponsored by the National Australia Bank, at which I was to talk about reading aloud. At the cocktail party beforehand I found myself standing with two soberly dressed bank managers, both in their late thirties. I ascertained that they were both fathers of young sons.

"Guys, you do read aloud to your kids, don't you?" I said. "I'll have to kill you if you don't!"

"Too right I do," said the first. *"Hairy Maclary from Donaldson's Dairy."* And the second said, quoting from Lynley Dodd's brilliant book: "Hercules Morse as big as a horse with Hairy Maclary from Donaldson's Dairy." And the first said: "Bottomley Potts covered in spots, Hercules Morse as big as a horse and Hairy Maclary from Donaldson's Dairy." Unbelievably they stood there together in their black suits and proper ties and did an impromptu recital of the entire book! It was hysterical and certainly proved that they'd read that wonderful book, if no other, over and over again to their lucky sons.

☆

Bank managers, politicians, business people, military personnel, and any other mothers and fathers whose working hours keep them from their children more than they would like, might think about taking a

selection of favorite books to work so if they're delayed or can't get home before the child goes to bed,
they can read a book over the phone as the child follows along at home. Parents away from home for long

stretches might like to videotape themselves reading aloud so their children can watch them telling stories night after night and not lose touch.

By now you'll have realized that I believe reading aloud cures pretty well everything from warts to global warming. But don't take my word for it. Find the nearest adored child and discover it for yourself.

☆

Twenty Books
That Children Love

The world and I could argue forever about what's left off this list. Hundreds of other wonderful books exist. These fail-safe suggestions are merely here for parents who need guidance to start with, before they bravely choose books on their own.

I Went Walking by Sue Machin,
illustrated by Julie Vivas

Each Peach Pear Plum by Janet and Allan Ahlberg

Brown Bear, Brown Bear, What Do You See?
by Bill Martin, Jr., illustrated by Eric Carle

Green Eggs and Ham by Dr. Seuss

Are You My Mother? by P. D. Eastman

Where the Wild Things Are by Maurice Sendak

Where's Spot? by Eric Hill

The Very Hungry Caterpillar by Eric Carle

Owl Babies by Martin Waddell,
illustrated by Patrick Benson

Hairy Maclary from Donaldson's Dairy
by Lynley Dodd

Rascal the Dragon by Paul Jennings,
illustrated by Bob Lea

Madeline by Ludwig Bemelmans

Wombat Stew by Marcia K. Vaughan,
illustrated by Pamela Lofts

Who Sank the Boat? by Pamela Allen

Dr. Seuss's ABC by Dr. Seuss

Dear Zoo by Rod Campbell

We're Going on a Bear Hunt by Michael Rosen,
illustrated by Helen Oxenbury

Rosie's Walk by Pat Hutchins

The Elephant and the Bad Baby by Elfrida Vipont,
illustrated by Raymond Briggs

*Alexander and the Terrible, Horrible, No Good, Very
Bad Day* by Judith Viorst, illustrated by Ray Cruz

☆

Acknowledgments

I owe a huge debt to Sue Williams and Jane Covern-ton, the divine publishers of my first book, *Possum Magic,* who urged me to write this book and thereby set the ball rolling. Also boundless, endless thanks to Jenny Darling, my beloved agent, who picked up the ball, ran with it, bounced it, and tossed it around with so much energy and efficiency that I felt quite faint watching it all from the sidelines. And finally infinite gratitude to my adored editor, Allyn Johnston, whose work on this book—without a single cross word—was so ruthless it made me breathless, so sublime it made me soar.